How To Raise your parents

How To Raise your parents

Gordon R. McLean

Tyndale House Publishers
Wheaton, Illinois

Coverdale House Publishers Ltd.
London and Eastbourne, England

Distributed in Canada by
Home Evangel Books Ltd.
Toronto, Ontario

Other books by Gordon R. McLean:

We're Holding Your Son
    Published by Fleming H. Revell Company

High on the Campus—Student Drug Abuse
    Haskell Bowen, Co-Author
    Published by Tyndale House Publishers

Readers interested in the work of Mr. McLean may
contact him at Campus Life, 1190 Lincoln Avenue,
San Jose, California 95125.

Second Printing, November 1970

Library of Congress Catalog Number 73-123288
SBN Number 8423-1525—X Cloth
8423-1526—8 Paper

Printed in the United States of America

Dedicated to
"Big Bufe" Karraker,
area vice-president of YFC Campus Life
in California,
who, despite the handicaps of being a parent,
is one of the best friends
teen-agers have.

CONTENTS

CONTENTS

FOREWORD

When I first picked up this book, its title jolted me. "How dare you?" I thought.

Yet by the time I had finished reading it, Gordy had won me over. We adults constantly have to fight the tendency to sell you teen-agers short. How often we parents hide behind custom, outside influences, face-saving, and even personal insecurity.

Actually, I should have learned by this time. Every year of my life since college has been invested in working with young people. Four of our six children have lived through their teen years, and our twins have just begun theirs.

Your straightforward honesty, teen-agers, forces me to reevaluate. I'm learning that it's good for me to occasionally acknowledge, "I was wrong." In fact, I'm finding it's much better to give the teen-ager the benefit of the doubt. Why shouldn't you have the privilege of my confidence until you prove otherwise?

I like you the way you are *now!* You welcome counsel, and even rules. Your rebellion is often against closed minds, premature judgment, and unreasonable demands.

Some of my most rewarding experiences have been in listening to teens like yourselves. Often, I have learned much from you even as I was helping you. You want it straight, and you want it honest.

That's why I can recommend this book. Gordy knows what he's talking about. He comes through strong because of his personal commitment to Christ and a vital, up-to-date involvement with hundreds of kids much like yourself.

SAM WOLGEMUTH

PREFACE

This may well be the first book written largely during a radio broadcast with the listeners calling in their comments, ideas, and suggestions, but that is how it came about.

Each Sunday night I talk with high school and college students on a phone-in show on KLIV radio in San Jose. When one caller suggested that there should be a book on all the problems between teens and parents, I said I'd be happy to write it. Other callers over the next several weeks suggested questions and topics to include in it. While all the audience is certainly not in agreement with my Christian convictions, they still were anxious to hear my opinions on the traditional areas of parent-teen problems — dating, cars, grades — as well as some more recent issues — protests, civil disobedience, and the new morality. This book is the result.

I wish to express my thanks to the following:

Dr. Sam Wolgemuth, the president of Youth for Christ International, who has been a great inspiration in heading up one of the most vital and effective youth movements in the world today;

HOW TO RAISE YOUR PARENTS

Jim Buchfuehrer, Ray Ramsey, and the YFC Campus Life staff here in the Santa Clara Valley who have done such a great job of ministry with our local teens; and David Coleman, director for Voice of Christian Youth in Tacoma, Washington;

The Board of Directors and many kind friends who so faithfully support and help us in the YFC Campus Life program;

Robert Nino, the dedicated and capable chief probation officer for the Santa Clara County Juvenile Court, whose kindness to and concern for the young people in his care is a constant inspiration;

Robert Kieve and the staff at KLIV who permitted me to turn a radio program into an author's workshop;

Ralph Thompson, the talented artist whose illustrations add so much to this material;

Campus Life magazine, for permission to use material from my articles as well as other quotes in this work;

Charles Chase who carefully edited this manuscript.

Dan Poley and his father for an interesting introduction;

The many teens and youth leaders whose ideas have come together in these pages.

While all of these friends have shared in this book, I must disclaim for them agreement with all the views expressed in these pages, for which I alone am responsible.

GORDON R. McLEAN

INTRODUCTION

by Dan Poley
with comments by Dan's father

I'm a teen-ager, and a book of suggestions on how to raise my parents just has to be appealing. (The only thing I have to watch is my dad getting the chance to put his comments beside mine.)

Truthfully, I'm more fortunate than the average teen-ager because I have a close relationship with my folks. They spend most of their time working with young people — my dad spent twenty-two years on active duty with the Air Force and is now science professor at a community college, and my mother teaches in elementary school. We do communicate with each other — we really do!

Not that there isn't an occasional ripple on our smooth waters. For example, can you see why two adults could possibly object to a ten-piece drum set sitting in the middle of their living room? It's not that I play them constantly; I do take time out to sleep. To make matters worse, my girl friend is on their side — she resents playing second fiddle to a set of Ludwigs.

>*There is another set of drums he should consider, eardrums. They can't be replaced!*

Speaking of musicians, the problem of my supposedly long hair comes up occasionally. I can't see why; I'm willing to go to a barber a couple of times a year whether I need a trim or not. What all this talk about hair boils down to is simply this: my dad is jealous.

>*The issue isn't really hair length — it's keeping the impulsiveness of youth within reasonable limits. I'm aware that a head of more than minimal length hair does not necessarily harbor a revolutionary. I do feel we have been able to arrive at a happy compromise with the choice really left to Dan.*

>*I'm not jealous about my son having more hair than I have — all great men come out on top! It was a real barb when Dan gave me a comb for Christmas and said, "You'll never be able to part with this, Dad."*

Then there's the problem of my social life. My parents want me to enjoy a well-rounded range of activities, but they don't want me to get too serious with one girl at my age. I want to go with one girl — one at a time, that is. I keep telling my parents teen-agers go steady for better or for worse, but not for long, so they shouldn't get shook. But we still don't see eye to eye on that. Can I help it if they're cross-eyed?

> *Undying love knows no bounds, but does it have to come at, say, age fifteen, and with one girl? Why not distribute the wealth a little more evenly to all?*

Now from the birds and the bees to the car and the keys. The little matter of the family car is where we come closest to a crisis, if not to open hostilities. In my modest way, I have to admit I'm pretty mature and responsible. Once in awhile I may get a little cocky behind the wheel, but I haven't had any wrecks or tickets — yet. Maybe if I got to drive more, the novelty would wear off. You see, between the number of nights each week I want the car and the number of nights my parents will let me use it, there is a range of exactly seven nights! I keep insisting to my dad even the Bible says he should let me use the car — "He that spareth the rod hateth his son" — but I think my dad has a different interpretation.

> *I do!*

I've tried many angles to convince him of the importance of my using the car, but I've come to the heartbreaking conclusion that the only way I'll solve the problem is to work and get my own car and insurance. How desperate can you get?

> *When a teen gets behind the wheel of a car the newfound feeling of adventure takes him beyond reasonable limits at times. It often cuts into study time as well. When my son shows his mother and me*

>*grades at school consistent with his ability, the privilege — and I emphasize privilege — of driving will be given to him.*

Despite any differences, there is something that keeps us together. Both my folks and I have a real commitment to Christ. That doesn't mean we just sit in a church pew on Sunday morning thinking about how quickly we can get out for dinner. Rather, the Lord is a real and personal part of our everyday lives. He helps us face any of the problems that come along, big or small, with love and understanding. Because of this, I feel a real close relationship with my folks.

>*We all have a responsibility for putting our faith to work in everyday situations. It's the duty of a parent to represent God in the raising of a child until that child finds a direct relationship with the Lord that supersedes his parents'. Then the parent can abrogate to a great extent the control he has over his child. The best controls are not external, but those which a young person builds within his own life!*

Another close friend of mine is the author of this book, Gordon McLean. I met him early in my high school days and we spent a lot of time together. He opened up a whole world of opportunities and service for me as a young Christian. Through YFC Campus Life Club at our school I've had the privilege of sharing my faith in Christ with other kids on campus. Through my participation in numerous Youth for Christ musical groups, helping produce

Teen Line on KLIV radio, and working with guys my own age at the county juvenile ranch, I have had even more opportunities to share my faith. I've found serving the Lord to be neither dull nor boring.

I've mentioned some of the things that annoy me. You may have other things bugging you — sex, insecurity, military service, protests, your future — all hang-ups between you and your parents.

Here, in this book, you'll get much of the help you need to get your parents (and you) through the most difficult period of their life, your teen-age years.

DAN POLEY

Just a closing comment for my son. Dan, be very careful where you leave your copy of this book. Some day your own children may get it out and have a wealth of arguments to use on you. Good luck!

George Poley

1

The Care and Feeding of Parents

I was once introduced at a meeting as "California's oldest teen-ager." I thought at first it was a reference to my I.Q., but as the introduction continued I was relieved to learn the remark was related to my spending considerable time listening to and working with teen-agers.

In all frankness, I must tell you that an American teen-ager is something I have never been. I was born and raised in Canada, lived my late teen years in the United States, and became an American citizen when I was twenty-three. My friendship with American youth has been by choice, and I find you the most exciting, intelligent, friendly, and eager people I could possibly imagine. I've spent all of my adult life getting to know you — I've shared your joys, your fun, your heartbreaks, your tragedies, your hopes, your disappointments; I've laughed with you and cried with you.

Unlike many adults, I've listened to you — often in private counseling sessions or in groups of two or three — and I've heard your views on every conceivable subject when for years each Sunday night we've talked over the phone on the radio with thousands sharing our conversations. When we've met personally you've shared confidences you'd never tell your folks or any other adult. I know a good deal about what bothers you.

I've never been naive enough to suggest I know all the answers to your questions — I'm still trying to find many of my own. But I do have some experience and some convictions, and when I get stuck I have available some excellent resources from whom to get help. Without trying to ram anything down your throat, I will speak firmly on those things I believe to be right. You, in turn, have every right to disagree.

I know how you feel about adults. You'd like to relate to most of them, especially those closest to you. Sometimes you are frustrated in knowing how, so, in desperation, you withdraw.

In a recent survey at Michigan State University, 79 percent of the parents interviewed thought they communicated well with their kids; but 81 percent of the kids of these same parents said their parents were not successfully communicating with them.

I know how adults feel about you. Many of them have forgotten you are people and tend to take at face value everything they read in the press and magazines about teen-agers — much of which is utter nonsense. They believe there is something called a Generation Gap. You know it isn't true, but you are not above using *their* belief in it now and then to gain your own ends. All teen-agers aren't alike any more than all adults are. If there's a gap, it is between people. You don't relate to some adults, but you don't have much in common with everyone your own age either. Parents who tell me they can't communicate with you have usually long since quit communicating with each other!

You feel adults are so busy saying things, they never stop to listen. They have become so used to doing all the talking that when you start to speak, they think you're wising off. Everything else in the modern household has a switch to turn it off and on — why don't children?

When I asked some of you at a youth conference what the major problems were in youth-parent, student-teacher relationships, you gave me these answers:

1. Parents are overprotective; they are afraid to let youth make mistakes in order to learn.

2. Some parents do not love or want the best for their children.

3. Parents are too selective in their communication. Too often they do not listen to the things young people want to discuss.

4. Adults are hypocritical. They set rules and legislate values for youth that they do not practice.

5. Teachers are often afraid to discuss important issues because they feel threatened by the administration, the school board, students, or parents.

6. Not enough parents and teachers are interested in the social issues that young people are interested in.

You also gave these suggestions for how some of these problems might be met:

1. Adults should spend more time listening and trying to understand youth.

2. More counselors and teachers need to take

more time to discuss current issues and personal problems with students.

3. You want a voice and a role in those agencies making decisions that affect your lives — school, community, and church. You are eager to have representatives on community planning councils, recreation committees, and church boards; and you don't see how these agencies can really act in your best interest until you do.

But all of these problems and your ability to cope with them center in your relations with two people, your mom and dad. And it is here you often have your greatest frustrations and need the most help. The "care and training" of your parents may well be your most difficult assignment as a teen-ager.

You've pointed out things your parents could do to get along better with you. Here were your key suggestions to mom and dad:

1. Listen to your teen when he disagrees with you. Don't do all the talking and tell him to shut up.

2. Assure your teen that you trust him.

3. Be courteous to your teen's friends, and make them feel welcome.

4. Be big enough to say, "I made a mistake; I'm sorry."

5. Show your teen you love him; don't be embarrassed to express your affection.

6. Don't compare your teen with a brother or sister or a neighbor or a relative who does better.

7. Keep your promises to your teen.

8. Praise your teen when he does something that

deserves praise; don't just criticize him when he does something wrong.

9. Set a good example in your personal honesty.

10. Use the kind of language in front of your teen you want him to use.

Know what you as a teen-ager are up against? The fact that your parents have been around longer than you and are responsible for your being here gives them incalculable advantages, including the idea that they know more than you do. And they do. It's how they press that advantage that causes the rift. They can get unbearable.

They dislike your music, consider your friends creeps or worse, check your time in with a stopwatch, suspect you of all manner of evil doings, gape at your wardrobe, insist your room be cleaned when it's much easier for you to find things the way it is, resent your tying up the phone line, limit your use of the car — in fact, it's a wonder you've been able to survive this long under such tyranny!

When you're just being normally impulsive, you're told, "Why don't you grow up? Why, you're practically an adult. You should act like one."

So when you respond by showing some independent judgment, you're squelched with, "Now we'll decide that for you. After all, you're still young and we know what's best for you." You can't win.

Of course not all parents are that bad — some are worse.

But even if you never fully understand how mom and dad reason, the point is that you must make the effort. You are confronted with the Bible's statements, "Honor your father and mother," and

"Obey your parents in all things; for this is well pleasing unto the Lord." There is an interesting verse right after that last one that doesn't get quoted as often — I wonder why? It says, "Fathers, provoke not your children to anger, lest they be discouraged." Good advice — *all* of it.

Your parents insist they love you. But there are times when you wonder, especially when they want to prove that love by limiting the things you do. Why, you've at least three sources for guidelines which you think are better than your parents' standards, and you'll be glad to tell them —

"Look, dad, *anybody* knows better than that — you're just not with it!"

Or, "Come on now, mom, *nobody* does that anymore — that's really out of it."

And finally, "It isn't really so bad. *Everybody* is doing it now — it's really in."

So there are your three authorities — *anybody, nobody*, and *everybody*. Great crew.

Just as you may find it easier to give in than to stand up to the crowd, I'm sure your folks would find it much more pleasant at times to just go along with you. When their experience and judgment tell them something is wrong or dangerous for you, they may not always be right; but remember, they are taking the difficult road, and they are doing it because they really care.

*   *   *   *

Perhaps it is wise to remind you that good parents are developed, not born. Kids today, more than ever before, have to have finely developed skills if they are going to succeed in raising good parents. Here are a few suggestions:

1. *Encourage them.* Many parents are insecure in a world that is new to them, and they are often confused and hesitant. You can encourage their hobbies. Don't harp on embarrassing fine points such as telling them the bank called to say the checking account was overdrawn. Things like that are better left for them to find out by themselves. Unless parents are allowed to make mistakes, they are never going to learn to fend for themselves.

2. *Set a good example for adults by staying away from alcohol and tobacco.* Adults tend to copy the language, styles, and tastes of the young — it's the only reasonable substitute for finding the fountain of youth — so the example you set is very important. Sneaking off to drink was a big deal when they were growing up, and nobody had yet linked cigarette smoking to lung cancer; so many adults have fallen prey to both habits. Without being overly critical, encourage their abstinence by setting a good example.

3. *Be concerned over their outside activities.* Insist your parents bring their friends home so you can meet them. Ask for references such as credit cards so you can be assured they're not running with the wrong crowd. Be sure they get to bed at a reasonable hour, especially on week nights.

4. *Carefully watch their activities in the home.* The effects of television on adults has not yet been fully established, but certainly there is plenty of cause for concern. Daytime dramas are much too strong for the average mother, and fathers may not

be up to watching the displays of violence and sex. Either might prove damaging.

5. *Don't be too strict with your parents.* Many parents suffer from overly strict children who keep them subdued with harsh discipline. Then the parent breaks the chain, rebels, and strikes out against a society they feel is alien to their needs.

Parents must have leeway. They should have access to the phone, the stereo, and the car — under carefully spelled out conditions, of course.

Each parent is unique, with his own set of problems. Even good kids, if they are not conscientious, may find themselves raising disturbed parents. Parents' problems usually go back many years, and are not going to be solved in one day.

Dr. Charles Shedd, author of *The Stork Is Dead* adds some very impressive points for you to consider on your side of the fence:

Remember, you're no bargain to live with either. If there's one thing tougher than being a teen-ager, it's having one.

Remember, nobody gets everything he wants. Others have their wants and ideas too.

Let them have their way sometimes, especially with the little things. If you show you are willing to give in some of the time, they are more likely to cooperate when it's some big deal you've just got to have.

Show a little sympathy. "Understanding" is a good word for bettering any relationship. Try to see things through your parents' eyes.

Say "thank you" to each of your folks at least once each day. They'll survive the shock, and when they do, they'll be bragging everywhere about their wonderful teen-ager.

At least once each week, do something nice for your parents. You might give them a night out while you stay home and baby-sit — the key here is to offer before being asked.

Learn how to say "I'm sorry." Few things can lift the level of human relations like honest humility properly expressed.

Never do anything to betray their trust or make them question your honesty. When your folks lose faith in you and it's your fault, you've lost a whole bunch.

Try to work up agreements which will eliminate some arguments in advance. Things like allowance, work around the house, use of the telephone — these can all be settled ahead of a crisis.

Ask their advice now and then on something big enough to make them feel important. There is hardly a parent alive in sound mind who wouldn't react favorably to these four words, "I need your help."

Tell them you'd like to know about sex straight from them. Many parents would like to try to discuss sex with their children. If you'd only prompt them a little, maybe they wouldn't do half bad.

Communicate. Life will be a whole lot better if *you* make the effort to communicate — don't just leave it to them.

Meanwhile, you can help by living your own life the best you can. Some teens get so upset over the shortcomings of mom and dad they don't notice their own. But, after living in a difficult family, you may need some help yourself to get on a sound footing. Don't hesitate to go to a pastor, youth director, or counselor for the help you need.

One of the cruelest forms of neglect is practiced by parents who never say no to their own children, who don't care enough to require what is right from them. The chances are overwhelming your parents *do* know what is right and best for you.

But still you have a problem of communication — getting them to listen to your views and your problems.

Part of it may be your fault. Begin by picking an appropriate time for discussions. The night your dad announces losing the biggest business deal of the year is not the time to say, "I'm really sorry, dad; and by the way, the smashed rear end of your car that I wrecked this afternoon won't take more than a week to fix. I hope you're not upset." He's apt to be.

Try to find a time when your parents are neither upset nor hurried. If you approach them with sincerity, courtesy, and respect — the same qualities you want when they talk with you — you're apt to get a good, fair hearing. It's a real pleasure for parents to know their youngster has enough trust in them to come to them.

Take mother and dad into your confidence. Put as much effort into being friends with your folks as you do into your friendships at school. Remember, parents are human. They'll respond to kindness.

I know being a teen-ager is not the easiest job in the world, but being a parent is no cinch either. News commentator Paul Harvey says, "Being a parent is the last hold-out of the amateur. Every other job requires education and training but this one. And by the time you learn from experience and become an expert, the job is done!"

Pity the poor father who said, "I don't know what to do with my teen-ager son. I can't tell him anything; he knows more than I do. I can't hit him; he's bigger than I am. I can't bribe him; he's got more money than I have!"

You worry about your parents trusting you. Let's turn that around. *You* trust people who have proved to you that your confidence in them is well placed — who keep their word, keep your confidences, and are dependable. They have earned your trust.

You must earn the same trust — and your conduct says a great deal more than your insistent demands for confidence. Trust doesn't come in a day or two, especially after some disappointments and failures; but if you'll be patient, it will come.

Sometimes your parents are concerned about your choice of friends. They may have reason. If your boy friend has all the neatness, manners, and attitudes typical of an outlaw motorcycle gang member, you may have trouble finding him a warm welcome at your house. A little extreme perhaps, but the point is there.

Your parents want you to associate with the kind of people who will contribute to your future success and happiness. And when they do turn thumbs down on a particular association, it's not your fun they're considering — it's your future, even if you don't recognize it.

There may be a conflict here; friendship, like love, is often blind, and parents are cautious. But if that fellow doesn't think enough of you to look and act decently around you and your parents, to meet them courteously, and to treat them with respect, then your parents are right! Trade him in for a better model.

It's all part of the battle for maturity and independence. A young lady named Kate writes to her parents in *Focus on Youth*:

"I want you to care about me as a person, about the person I'm becoming. Sometimes I get the feeling you only are concerned about how I make you look to your friends. I know that pretty soon I am going to be out on my own, but it hurts when you say, 'As long as you're living in our house you do as we say. As soon as you're on your own you can do anything you want.' It makes me feel like you're just waiting to kick me out and you don't really care what happens to me after I'm away and my behavior no longer reflects on you. If you're really making decisions for my well-being, then you have to care just as much about what happens to me after I'm out on my own. Do you understand what I mean? When I get the feeling you only care about how I act in relation to you, I lose respect for you. It seems like you're more worried about being a 'good parent' than you are about what's happening inside of me."

However much your parents may say they can hardly wait for you to grow up and be out on your own, it appears they may not really mean it and, in fact, suffer ill effects when you do leave. A growing number of marriages break up when the last child is ready to leave home — after the parents have been married twenty years or more. Dr. Alfred Messer, professor of psychiatry at Emory University, points out, "We are living in the century of the child, where the children become a nucleus around which most activities revolve." Child-oriented parents, who man endless car pools for school and oversee club meetings and camp-outs, look to their children for emotional gratification. In some cases, communication between parents is carried on primarily through the children. When the kids leave, and a void ensues, the parents cannot satisfy or readjust to each other.

How does this affect you now? Dr. Messer says that young people, thrust into the role of helping fulfill the needs of their parents, are not free to develop their own personalities. Equally injurious is the image of marriage impressed upon the child. It is seen as a strained, unloving, and frustrating trap.

We're just getting started. There's lots more to talk about that separates the generations in this space age, and we've got many things to consider together if you're going to help your parents survive your teen-age years.

2

"Hey, Dad, Can I Use the Car?"

The phrase "step on it" never really came into its own until teen-agers discovered automobiles — or was it some Russian named Fordovsky? At any rate, getting your parents to understand the vital importance of a car in today's world presents all sorts of pitfalls.

You may encounter the discouraging belief that there should be definite limitations on your use of the family's go-wagon, or worse still, the prevailing idea may be that you should wait until you can afford —

1. a car of your own,
2. the insurance,
3. the gas.

Suppose you just can't get a car at all? Then what?

First, you'll give your girl an opportunity to prove it's you, and not the car, she really loves.

Second, you might find it a real boost to your budget and to your education. Interestingly enough, one high school found that very few straight-A students owned a car, but 83 percent of the guys failing did!

But suppose you do get to use the car, or you have your own. Then maybe you have the problem of convincing your parents to let you keep using it and not to worry about you. How you operate behind the wheel tells the story here.

At the moment we in America have the ignoble distinction of having killed and injured more people on our highways than we have in all of our wars. Automobile insurance rates have skyrocketed for the accident-prone teen-age group to an almost impossible high. But still our highway accident figures climb.

Insurance companies, the police, and National Safety Council officials (assisted for a long while by the Burma Shave Company) have racked their collective brains to make all of us realize the danger of steering several hundred horsepower at tremendous speeds on superhighways.

Have you heard these tidbits?

> "He always insisted on the right-of-way;
> So did the ambulance that took him away."

> "He came to a railroad and didn't stop to hear;
> Death didn't draft him, he was a volunteer."

> "He thought that proper distance was bunk
> Till they pulled him out of some guy's trunk."

> "He passed on curves and thought it was funny;
> His widow is spending the insurance money."

An offended teen complains, "We're tired of slams at young drivers. Many of us are a lot less of a menace on the highway than some of our elders." Granted. As one police officer remarked, "The trouble isn't just those under twenty-one going over sixty. It's also people over sixty going under twenty-one!"

I'll gladly point up the good being done to promote traffic safety by high school driving courses, touring groups such as the Spurrlows for Chrysler Corporation, teen driving contests, and safety-minded car clubs all over the nation. That doesn't change the fact, though, that we still have to con-

vince some young drivers that show-off tactics behind the wheel are hard on a teen's reputation, his
pocketbook, and his life expectancy.

Before some fellow brings it up — it isn't all
women drivers either. National statistics indicate
that women are safer behind the wheel than men.

To test this out, our YFC Saturday night program sent a teen-age fellow and girl out in identical
cars, supposedly to notice the driving habits of others. A "friend" went along with each of them to
take notes. The "friends" were plainclothesmen,
and they reported back to the rally on how our
two kids had driven. The result: a victory for the
girl. The boy, with some thirteen violations noted,
could have been fined a total of $125. In the inter-
ests of safety, you girls might insist on driving on
all dates from now on!

Two researchers at the University of Michigan discovered some interesting characteristics of male
drivers age fifteen to twenty-five who were involved
in serious accidents. First, they discovered the dangerous driver likes to drive for fun, is proud of how
his car looks and takes good care of it, drinks and
will drive after drinking, speeds inside city limits,
races other cars, has occasional fist fights, drives to
blow off steam, resents adult pressures and discipline, has older brothers and sisters, is likely to come
from a laboring-class family, and has (or had) low
grades in school.

The authors of the study noted that during the
ten-year span in which the young person is moving
from adolescence to adulthood, he is struggling to
become an adult but is not yet granted that privi-

lege by society. Ego and virility seem to be the factors that prompt the male driver to do many foolish things behind the wheel of a car.

A healthy mixture of responsibility and practical sense could do a lot for the driving habits of all of us. Let's throw in a few tips.

Traffic laws are to be obeyed, not treated as a challenge. That sign reading "35 MPH" doesn't mean 70 just because there are two of you.

Learn all you can about how to handle your car in emergencies. Don't just trust luck. Be aware of braking distance and possible mechanical failures. Keep your car in good shape. There's a lot to a car. There are several thousand nuts in a car — the most important of which is behind the steering wheel! (We couldn't resist that!)

Fast driving belongs on a drag strip, not on a public highway. The highway may be marked in lanes ideally suited for competition, but this is not to be taken as a public invitation to proceed. Racing on the open road is neither fun nor funny. Races often end up in another race — to get the participants to the hospital while they're still breathing.

Plain impatience is also risky. You know the kind of driver who honks the horn the instant a light turns green, or who weaves in and out of fast-moving traffic. Another source of trouble is the driver who can spare only one arm for the steering wheel because the other one is around his date. Look, guys, one hand may be all right for a forward pass or throwing a curve ball; but when it comes to driving, keep both hands on the wheel.

Seat belts have proved effective in saving lives,

but they won't if they're not used. What's *your* excuse?

You can probably take it from here; but remember, safe driving is a moral responsibility just like any other act of good citizenship.

From a fellow who drives a lot, to all of you: happy motoring, and please be careful. The life you save may be mine!

3

"I was WONDERING About..."

It's exciting to exchange views with the high school crowd. In addition to meeting students on campus and talking to them over the air, I often meet them for several days at conferences. These are particularly enjoyable events because they provide opportunity to get better acquainted and often give me the chance to use an anonymous question box from which I can take and discuss questions the students raise.

Naturally these students don't always agree with my views, which is fine. It's not conformity I'm after; if I can stimulate some thinking and provide a few guide lines for a teen-ager to use in getting his own answers, I'm well satisfied.

Here, selected at random, are some recent questions along with my replies:

There's this boy I like a lot, and we've been going steady for about a year. My parents think I should go out with other fellows, but I want to stay with this one boy. Do you see anything wrong with that?

Perhaps the best way to handle this question would be to begin by asking another question. Why do you go steady? Here are some of the reasons teens go steady. Which, if any, fits your situation?

1. You like the security of having a well-trained, ready-made date on hand — sort of a teen-age form of social security.

2. You actually go more steadily than steady — you have several steadies at the same time, so you're never left hanging.

3. (Girls) You want to reform or mother him. (You'll find you can do that job better as a friend than as a date.)

4. You like the feeling of domination. "This girl is mine. All mine." "My boy friend always does anything I want."

None of these reasons reflects a mature, intelligent relationship between two people who respect each other. They hinge on fear, frustration, and weakness. Here are a couple of other factors to consider before you decide to go steady:

1. How will you ever know if this is really "the one" if you don't go out with others?

2. You may get really interested in someone else who comes along, but the switch may be painful if you're tied down. As the old song says, "Breaking up is hard to do," so why invite an emotional tearjerker for the last act?

3. Be sure you're ready before you go steady. Familiarity leads to intimacy — why put yourself in the place of temptation?

Conclusion: why not be wise and socialize?

I've got a real problem with my parents. They're the CIA, FBI, and Secret Service all rolled up into

*one. I'm in the tenth grade and my parents always
sneak around to find out where I've been, who I'm
dating, checking when I get in. It's a real drag.
How can I get my parents off my back? My boy
friend is really hurt because his parents trust him
and never ask what he's doing.*

My first thought is to wonder what you've done
that makes your parents distrust you and makes you
so concerned about their finding out. Trust is something you earn, not demand.

But even if your slate is clean, don't ascribe sin-
ister motives to your folks. They love you, and they
want to share and enjoy to some degree your teen-
age experiences.

So don't force them to sneak around to find out
about your activities. Tell them before they ask.
Be sure they know the boy who is taking you out.
Tell them where you're going, be in on time (call
if you are delayed), and share some of the high-
lights of a fun evening with them when you return
— and also the disappointments.

I think your parents are showing a great deal
more love for you than are the parents of the boy
who don't care enough to find out where he is or
what he is doing. Juvenile hall is filled with kids
whose parents never bothered to find out what their
kids did — until it was too late.

*If I don't let him kiss me on the first date, will he
ever ask me out again?*

Despite some evidence to the contrary, kisses
handed out as free samples are not highly regarded.
They are still supposed to mean something. Some

good advice: never let a kiss fool you or a fool kiss you.

There's something intriguing and special about being less than available. But you don't need to go to the other extreme so the boy thinks he's dating an iceberg. Assembly speaker Don Lonie noted that some of the best advice on dating for girls is found on the top of a mayonnaise jar: Keep cool but don't freeze.

Everything was going fine until my parents found out my boy friend had been in juvenile court and is now on probation. He's really learned his lesson and is a nice guy — a lot nicer than many of the guys who never got caught. But my parents forbid him to come to our house and won't let me date him any more.

I can understand the reluctance of your parents to welcome with open arms a boy who, they suspect, plays cops and robbers with real cops. But I'll take the facts you've given me at face value and hope your liking for the boy hasn't made you blind to his faults. I'll assume he's a changed man.

That's not hard for me to assume, by the way. I've worked with and known many hundreds of teen-agers who have been through court and institutional experiences. Many of them, including some who in the past were committed to correctional institutions for very serious offenses, are among my closest friends. A fellow (or girl) who has been in serious trouble and learned his lesson is often a stronger and a better person than a fellow who did the same things and was never caught. I would be the first to urge giving the boy a chance to prove himself, and I have argued this very position with many reluctant parents.

You may not be able to do much about the situation now because your parents are pretty set in their views — and largely because you and the boy handled it wrong in the first place. It's too bad your parents "found out" about his being in trouble. There was a much better route to go; they should have been told — by him. That would not have been easy, but if he really cared enough for you to invite you to date him regularly, he should have talked with your family. If he had sat down and told them about his situation and they could have seen from his attitude and manner he was a gentleman, the chances are they would have accepted him as that and there would have been no problem.

There is, of course, the possibility they would have been unwilling to accept him. Better it be done at that stage, though, than in an emotional scene later on.

But more than likely they would have accepted him. Again, experience with hundreds of families shows me the percentage of acceptance is very high when parents are told the truth. I've seen parents really go out of their way to be kind to the young man involved and become his strongest defenders.

If he's as fine a boy as you say, I hope he has enough wisdom to use this approach in the future.

I've read a lot about Christ's birth and then about his later life and death. Do we know anything about

HOW TO RAISE YOUR PARENTS

His teen-age years? I'm interested because maybe what I could learn about His teen life could help me with mine.

The authentic source on the life of Christ, the Bible, contains only one sentence dealing directly with the Lord as a teen-ager — "And Jesus increased in wisdom and stature, and in favor with God and man" (Luke 2:52). As Christ matured, He developed in every area of life — the physical, mental, social, and spiritual. To live a successful, balanced life you have to mature in each of those same areas.

Christ, as a normal teen-ager, faced the same battles you face, but He lived a dynamic, successful life. You can have the same power in your life that He had when He walked this earth as a man.

Here's the pattern: "Present your bodies . . . holy and acceptable unto God" — the physical; "Be not conformed to this world" — the social; "Be ye transformed by the renewing of your mind" — the mental; ". . . that ye may prove what is that good and acceptable and perfect will of God" — the spiritual. This is from Rom. 12:1 and 2 — again the need to develop each area of your life.

The physical includes everything relating to your body — from your appearance to your health to your sex drive.

The mental area involves your thoughts, your diligence in your studies, and your motivations.

The social area deals with your associations, your leadership, and your other abilities or talents.

The spiritual area is concerned with the place

you give to the Word of God, prayer, obedience, and your witness in sharing your faith.

A teen seeking to develop his life fully needs some encouragement. Your pastor, church, and related youth activities can be a much-needed boost. On a growing number of high school campuses in many parts of the world there are clubs designed to encourage the development of the balanced life. One of these is the Campus Life Club sponsored by Youth for Christ.

The Campus Life philosophy is "to develop in the Christian teen-ager a physical, mental, social, and spiritual balance that will enable him to properly and successfully communicate in word and deed his faith in Jesus Christ to his campus, to his friends, and to his world."

The club program has two phases: *Insight* — where Christian teens can share common problems and concerns and come up with practical, biblical help to meet those needs; and *Impact* — usually meeting in the evening in a home near the school, where the crowd from campus can enjoy an informal evening of fun, skits, and music. It ends with either a discussion or short talk by one of the staff, designed to present an interesting introduction to the Christian life.

Sound like a great teen-age program? It is! If you'd like to get more information on the Campus Life Clubs, you can write to: Campus Division, Youth for Christ International, Box 419, Wheaton, Illinois, 60187.

I go to a high school where there is quite a bit of

*racial tension. My parents are really worried about
the unrest, mainly because they can't figure out
what is happening. I don't know what to think.
When I tell mom and dad I want to see my black
friends get the same breaks I've had and that I don't
care who lives next door, they get all shook up.
We're a Christian family but are mighty confused.
What do you think?*

Uncertainty and fear go hand in hand, and what
your folks are going through is typical of the mood
of the whole country.

What most blacks want is simply to be treated
like other people, to enjoy equal treatment in the
courts, to vote, to go to good schools, to be equipped
for and get a good job, to be able to live anywhere
their means will allow — in short, to be full partners in America. They want black culture and
customs recognized and made a part of the educational program. They want you to know and appreciate them as people — black people. And they
don't want to wait; they feel they have waited long
enough. Waiting only strengthens the hold of the
ghetto and widens the gap economically between
them and the rest of the community.

Blacks don't understand your church which still
makes Sunday morning the most segregated time
of the week. They are baffled by your sending gen-
erously of your money and missionaries to an Af-
rican outpost while you ignore the racial minorities
at your doorstep and make plans to build your
new church in the suburbs when that minority gets
too large.

Whose problem is it? Whitney Young of the Urban League comments: "The real estate man or builder says the problem is economic; businesses and employers say the problem is one of education; and the educators say the problem is a matter of housing." It's all of these and more.

Governments, laws, and money alone will not solve America's race problems, although all three will have to be involved until our consciences catch up with reality. We, as believers, have a serious responsibility in a torn society to be what Paul called "agents of reconciliation," a task we can never fulfill if we maintain mistrust and hate, if we build walls instead of bridges to people, if we are not willing to recognize economically and socially that "of him to whom much has been given, much will be required." The average man in the community worries about his material things and his security, but a follower of the Lord should move from security to opportunity and be a healing force in a society that is sick.

Let me suggest two good books for you on the Christian and race relations: *My Friend, The Enemy* by Bill Pannell and *Black and Free* by Tom Skinner.

My parents and I constantly disagree over record albums and music I like to hear on the radio. Your talk show is heard on a Top Forty station. Do you think all the music today is evil and bad?

A prevalent adult idea is that almost all the music emanating from a contemporary station is somehow immoral, with innuendos of free sex and encouragement of drug use. There are many such songs, but there are also a good number that encourage straight living and healthy social concern. Adults who say all popular music is demon controlled are overgeneralizing. If adults call the art form of rock music unfamiliar or strange to their ears — okay. But they can't prove it is intrinsically evil. Things aren't evil; people are. If there is evil in music, it is because a person has sought to use it for evil goals. Sometimes adults are victims of journalists who carefully point out only the dirt.

Rock musicians may appear objectionable because of their long hair, their use of four-letter words, and their unacceptable philosophies of life. Parents experience a cultural shock as much as a moral one when they look at current rock stars. Parents often fear their son or daughter is going to identify with this person whose morals are bad, overlooking the fact that you can understand a man is a sinner without dwelling with him in sin.

John Fischer, a college student and musician, made some pertinent comments in a *Campus Life* magazine discussion: "Christian parents don't need to lay out lines and restrictions on what we can or can't listen to. Instead, they need to bring us up with an inner knowledge of Jesus Christ that will guide us to determine for ourselves what is right and wrong. If a parent lays down a bunch of rules, eventually the kid is going to find out that something prohibited is really lots of honest fun — and then he'll chuck the whole system. He has to learn how to make decisions himself under the direction of Christ, so that he has strength within himself."

Bev Pelton was part of the same discussion group. She plays guitar in a folk duo and said: "I can see where some songs have bad effects; I can pick out the wrong things while I'm listening, and some are really terrible. I say to myself, 'Now I've heard this song before; I know what it says and I know it's wrong.' Making this decision strengthens me."

And Linnea Sauter, a college student from Park Ridge, Illinois, who toured Europe with a Youth for Christ Teen Team, commented: "I used to think I was losing myself to something other than Christ. But music is a gift from God, a gift He has given for communication. I, as a supposedly mature Christian, must decide for myself what I listen to and why. Is it for music, for some sort of art I appreciate, or is it to get words that turn me on, that excite me, influence me wrongly?"

I have a friend who played for several years in a nationally known rock recording group. He had been only a nominal Christian, but the pressures of life on the road and exposure to the seamy side of life brought him face to face with his need for a deep spiritual commitment. He made it and unhesitatingly spoke of it. He had to live with the misunderstanding of many Christian people who were shocked by his appearance, his group, and their music. His own family subjected him to ridicule, but in the face of all the misunderstanding he quietly grew in his commitment. Today he is still in music work, although not with the same group, and is still firm in his stand for the Lord. He enjoys open doors of opportunity for witness to his faith that few of us will ever have. His pattern of life may not be that which all of us would choose to follow, but why should we condemn him?

Yes, there are a good many questions to be raised about contemporary music, and I've asked most of them at one time or another. It is so much easier to be totally against something like rock music than it is to be honest enough to look behind the rhythm and the beat to many songs asking some worthwhile questions and saying some worthwhile things.

You'll have to make some choices about your music — just as you do when you stand in front of a magazine rack or a book table or when you switch on your television set. A Christian has to make his decisions based upon his moral standards and the convictions he has from the Word of God. I don't think we can legislate music out of our lives. Instead we have to recognize it for what it is — the language of youth today. Christians must evaluate — then we can switch the dial when necessary to avoid letting our minds feed on junk.

I know a boy who uses marijuana and reds, (Seconal tablets, a barbiturate). *I want to help him, but I don't want to get him busted by the police. What should I do?*

I appreciate your concern for your friend, and I'm glad you want to help him. There are several things you can do, short of calling the police. Consider the whole situation and your own relationship with the boy, then perhaps try one or more of these suggestions:

1. You might try talking with him yourself. If you have enough influence on him and he respects

you, you might be able to get across the possible complications he faces from his use of "grass."

2. There might be a sympathetic adult whom both of you like and trust — a school counselor, teacher, youth director, pastor, or doctor. You could talk with that person and have him talk to the boy, knowing that this friend would respect both your confidence and that of the boy.

3. *If* you know his parents and *if* you know they are reasonable people who will try to help their son, you might talk to them.

4. There may be a community counseling agency or clinic that deals with the drug abuse problem and to whom you could go for help. Again, teachers, pastors or doctors should be able to direct you to any such local agencies.

You can get more information on various aspects of the drug problem and teen-age life from the book *High on the Campus,* which I've written with Haskell Bowen.

My parents are divorced, and I chose to live with my dad who is now remarried. My new stepmother and I just don't get along, and it's getting worse. I really like my dad, but I don't know how much more I can take from her. Should I live with my real mother or go to a foster home?

Your situation points out again how much easier it is for husbands and wives to shed mates than it is for youngsters to exchange parents. I have one young friend who is now on his fourth stepfather. He doesn't like his latest father very well, but he's hoping number five will be an improvement. That's a true situation, by the way, not a joke.

I think that what has happened here is that you felt a closeness to your father which, with a new adult coming into your home, has — at least in your mind — been threatened. Your stepmother, in turn, may not have enjoyed getting you as part of the deal when she married your father. The key to the solution will be what your father does. You ought to have a frank talk with him and let him know your feelings and anxiety. Loving both you and your new mother, perhaps he can mend the feelings.

Remember that your father is going to have to live his life long after you've left home, so don't be selfish and allow your feelings to destroy the new family. I have no way of measuring the depth of your problem and the feeling between you and your stepmother. If the problem is unsolvable in your home, then you may have to consider going to live with your mother, or a relative. Only as a last resort should you request foster home placement.

Keep this experience in mind because in a few years you will be looking forward to marriage and a home of your own. Remember that marriage is sacred and should be for keeps. I hope your generation, so many of whom know the tragedy of a broken home, will give much more care and consideration to setting up their own homes.

Which should I believe — science or the Bible?
Who says there's a conflict? The people who put science and the Bible at odds either don't know

their Bible or don't know their science. Listen to the comment of Dr. Werner von Braun of the National Aeronautics and Space Administration: "Science and religion are not antagonists. On the contrary, they are sisters. While science tries to learn more about the creation, religion tries to better understand the Creator. While, through science, man tries to harness the forces of nature around him, through religion he tries to harness the forces of nature within him . . . The better we understand the intricacies of the atomic structure, the nature of life, or the master plan for the galaxies, the more reason we have found to marvel at the wonder of God's creation."[1]

Dr. Kenneth N. Taylor has prepared two interesting books on science and faith: *Creation and the High School Student* and *Evolution and the High School Student*. Both are published by Tyndale House, Wheaton, Illinois.

Cheating on exams is rampant in our school. I don't want to do it, nor do I feel right about turning kids in for it. On the other hand, the cheaters make it harder on the student who is trying to do his best and get an honest grade. What should I do?

Cheating is prevalent in almost every high school; and the old excuse, "Everybody is doing it," is used to justify it. I found out from talking with students on Teen Line that it is often the better students, feeling the pressure for good grades and scholarships, who cheat. One fellow told me, "If you copy from

---

[1]From *This Week* magazine, copyright 1965 by United Newspapers Magazine Corporation.

one person, it's cheating; if you copy from three or four, it's research." When he went on to ask me what was really wrong with it I reminded him of the commandment, "Thou shalt not steal," and asked how he'd like to be operated on by a doctor who cheated his way through medical school!

You're right that cheating can make it rough on the kids who want to play it straight. Why don't you and several other students who share your views talk the problem over with the specific teacher in whose class it happens, or with a department head, or with the principal. Don't name names, just point out the problem, and request closer supervision during tests.

My parents think I should earn all my own spending money. Do you think this is right?
Yes.

4

"I Don't Get Nuthin' out of Church."

"Frankly, going to church is a bore," a sharp high school junior told me, giving vent to a view held in common by many of his crowd. "There are so many other things better than getting up for services — like sleeping. Besides, when I do go, I don't understand what they're talking about. I wish my folks would just let me forget the whole business!"

His eighth-grade brother summed it up still more simply: "I just don't get nuthin' out of church!"

Sound like a familiar tale of woe?

Let's be fair and look at the other side. While you may be quite eager to pass up church services for an extra hour in the sack, millions of teen-agers across the world can't worship freely at all. Perhaps if we lived in Eastern Europe, Russia, or in Red China, and had seen our churches closed, pastors imprisoned, and our Bibles burned, we'd put a higher value on religious freedom.

It might be good to remember the fastest way to lose a freedom — including freedom of worship — is to take it for granted or not use it at all.

True as this may be, it won't budge many kids. They still look at church-going as a waste of time or, at best, a polite deference to a family tradition of attendance far removed from the pattern of their daily lives. Forgive my enthusiasm, but I found as a high schooler that church can be inspiring, helpful, decidedly interesting, and even enjoyable — *if* you know the secret that makes it that way.

Here's what I'm getting at. Suppose I handed you a copy of the yearbook from a high school you were not acquainted with and suggested you read it. Chances are you'd scan it, glance at an interesting feature or two, and quickly cast it aside. You know why? Simple. You don't know the kids. On the other hand, you can hardly wait to see the next issue of your own high school yearbook and eagerly read it page by page — looking for familiar faces (your own first), events you remember, and activities of which you were a happy part.

The difference is in knowing the people it's all about. The same thing is true of the Bible and church. You'll get something from them when you know the person they're all about — Jesus Christ.

You show up for morning worship and the congregation sings, "He walks with me, and He talks with me, and He tells me I am His own" — a little stale if it has never happened to you. You drop in on the youth group and the gang is echoing, "Christ for me" — and it isn't Christ for you. At the evening service the crowd eagerly proclaims, "He lives within my heart" — but He doesn't live in yours. No wonder you don't get anything out of the services!

To many students Jesus Christ was just another figure in history: a great man, a noble teacher, a fine philosopher, an overeager religious zealot who came to a sad end on a Roman cross. Let's face it — it's a little hard to get worked up over Him if that's all He is. But take a second look. In the Bible, He made some far greater claims than those. He said, "He that has seen Me has seen the Father [God]" (John 14:9), and "I am the Way, the Truth, and the Life; no man approaches the Father but through Me" (John 14:6).

Are the claims of the Bible itself worth noting? Far from being the idle relic of mystic ancients or simply a record of history coupled with some good poetry and intriguing ethical principles it is, rather, as up-to-date as tomorrow's headlines. It has stood through several thousand years as the world's best-selling book because it has met the needs of men as only an inspired book could.

The claims of Jesus Christ are big claims. He says that He is God and that He is the only way to the truth of God. What can He produce to back up those statements? There's nothing worse than a man going around bragging about who he is, or what he can do, and then not being able to deliver the goods. What supports Christ's claim to being the Son of God? Far more than mere sentiment or tradition.

First, He hit history with such an impact that He split it in two. Even an atheist is forced to date his letters so many years after the coming of Christ.

Second, Jesus' birth, life, and death were foretold hundreds of years before His arrival. If God were sending His Son into the world, certainly He would announce the fact — and this was done! Throughout the Old Testament are details concerning the coming of the Savior of the world, all written many hundreds of years before Christ came!

Even aside from the Bible, the writings of many ancient historians and philosophers looked forward to the coming of a "King whom we must recognize to be saved," as Cicero recorded it. Pagan Tacitus in Rome predicted "a master and ruler of the world to come from Judea." Aeschylus, a Greek, in his *Prometheus*, declares, "Look for God to appear to accept upon his head the pangs of thy own sins." Even Plato and Socrates spoke of the "Universal Wise Man yet to come."

Then you can read in the New Testament how Christ was born, lived, ministered, and died — exactly as foretold! Now try this on Mohammed — who foretold his coming? or Buddha — who predicted where he'd be born? Confucius — who described the manner of his death centuries before he was born? Christ didn't just arrive on the scene and announce, "Listen to me." He was expected! This fact alone singles him out from every other religious leader the world has ever produced!

Third, Jesus came into the world to die. Every other religious leader was born, lived, taught, and died too. But that was the end of them. Death interrupted their careers, but not Christ's. If He were just a man, His death would have been a tragedy; being God, it became a victory. If He were merely human, the cross would have been a bitter scaffold; as God, it became a worldwide attraction!

Finally, Jesus' life — marked as it was by wise teaching, healing of the sick, and raising of the dead — does not fit the pattern of a mere good man. Good men don't lie! Christ claimed to be God in the flesh; and if He wasn't exactly what He claimed to be, then He certainly wasn't a good man. He was instead the greatest liar that ever lived!

Why did Christ come into this world and die an agonizing death by crucifixion? If he were the Son of God, couldn't He have avoided something so terrible?

Of course, but He chose to come and He chose to die in order to pay a debt. You see, God created man to have fellowship with Himself, and God gave man a free choice as to how He was going to live. To put it mildly, man goofed — a trend that has not changed noticeably since the days of creation. God, being a God of justice, required a death penalty for man's sin. Yet, being a God of love, He provided that payment in the death of His own son.

But Christ did not stop there. Three days later, He broke out of the tomb. He's not just in some far-off Heaven. He lives somewhere else, too. *He lives in the heart of every fellow and girl who opens the door of his or her life and invites Christ to come in.* It is this experience — called the "new birth" in John 3 — that makes a person a child of God.

What's involved? A recognition of the need in one's life, of your failures and sins, then a turning away from those things known to be wrong and a turning to Christ for forgiveness. God forgives you, and into your life comes divine strength day by day to make you the fellow or girl you ought to be. And at the end of this life comes an eternity with God forever. This is the experience of a fellow or girl

41

who is willing to allow Christ to take the central position in his life and have Him as the foundation of life.

If all this sounds like a pretty far cry from what most kids tend to think of Christianity — a lot of do's and don'ts — it is! Christianity isn't a code of rules; it doesn't require you to turn your back on life to become a religious hermit; nor does it entail going to a bunch of dead meetings. Rather it's a thrilling relationship with the Son of God that gives life meaning, power, and direction.

This relationship can be yours, too, if you'll pause long enough to invite Christ to come into your life. That experience will mean more and more to you as you get acquainted with the Bible, talk with the Lord, unite in the fellowship of a church, and share that faith with your friends.

Another very important aspect related to how much a teen-ager will appreciate his church is the quality of the program the church offers. Even the most spiritually enthusiastic young person will be turned off by a program that isn't turned on! Inadequate facilities, dull routines, boring programs, unskilled and inept leadership, irrelevant materials, uninteresting meetings — these are things that mark too many church youth programs and drive away teen-agers in droves. Believe me, I'm with you when you say it will take qualified leadership, adequate facilities and budget, and interesting, contemporary programs to attract you and your classmates to the church. Please don't confuse much of the insipid religious programming we see today with the exciting reality of a true spiritual experience.

Being a Christian isn't a ritual, but a reality.

Not form, but fact.

Not hoping, but knowing.

Not vague dreams, but genuine happiness.

Not quitting life, but truly finding it.

Not boredom, but purposeful living.

Not just going to meetings, but knowing a Person.

Once you find Him, He'll be with you wherever you are. You'll be glad to go to His house of worship, and you'll get more from it than you could ever imagine!

(P.S. You might even jump the gun and ask your parents to go with you!)

5

From D's to A's in Thirty Days

"That's all I hear. 'Got your homework done? How is your math coming? Have you studied for the history test?' It's terrible!"

"Anybody who talks about school as 'the good old days' must have had a mental lapse."

These kids, and probably you too, are feeling the pressure. Ever since the government gave national priority to the race for space, parents have been keeping a closer-than-ever eye on studies.

How do you handle the problem? The best way is keep your grades up. How do you do that though? First face the fact that good grades in school *are* important.

They provide you the satisfaction that comes from a job well done. And (believe it or not) you will actually be learning things in school that will be mighty important later in life.

You can't afford *not* to think of the influence those grades will have when you apply for college or other specialized training. All of the influence and pressure your pastor or friends and family can exert for you won't help in many schools if your scholastic record isn't up to par.

But there's another side of the problem that you ought to consider. You should be proving by your life, attitudes, and actions at school that spiritual commitment makes a wonderful difference in a person's life.

"Hold on now, pal. What has that got to do with grades?"

Plenty! How are you going to impress the kids in your school with the difference Christ makes if you take an indifferent attitude to your studies and if your marks are below theirs and below average? And if you are going to prove the validity of your faith, don't you think your parents and teachers ought to get generous helpings of the transformed you as well?

I have been thrilled many times when principals and teachers have told me: "These Christian teens are the best kids in school," or, "Those kids have a wonderful influence for moral living on our whole student body," and, "In these days when all too many young people seem to lack convictions we appreciate seeing young men and women in our school exerting a positive influence."

If that could be said of you, step up and take a modest but well-earned bow. And, believe me, the vast majority of young people like you are pitching in and doing a great job.

But there is the other side, sad to say. The teacher states: "I've got one of these church kids in my class, and his attitude sure isn't what it ought to be," or, "If she is going to be a leader in a Christian club, her work in class must be better."

Now, despite rumors to the contrary, our latest impartial national surveys indicate that teachers are human. When they back their attacks with facts, they have a case that is hard to beat. Face it squarely. Your influence is affected by the way you do your school work. If you're going to lead the singing at a club, plan the socials, and carry a Bible, you've got a responsibility to be the very best in all your activities, and that includes your class work. (Besides, aren't low grades an insult to your intelligence, which we automatically assume all readers to have?)

Now for the cod liver oil — sorry — we mean nice-tasting medicine. How can we produce a steady supply of report card Vitamin A? I have a formula (and the mere mention of that word should by now inspire your mathematical inclinations) which is absolutely guaranteed to produce the required improvement, or you are welcome to your old D's back!

Here is our miracle mark-maker method:

1. *Put the blame on the right person.* You won't get much in the way of permanent relief from your low grades by blaming the teachers or the subjects themselves. Sure, it would be nicer if reading, 'riting, and 'rithmetic were replaced with recess, refreshments, and roller-skating; but unless the modern trend in education is thrown completely overboard, that isn't likely to happen.

Besides (as the executioner said to the man in the electric chair, "This will shock you") there is value in many of those old subjects. Aside from the factual information which you may later use in surprisingly large quantities, such things as the increased ability to express yourself which comes from good use of proper English and training in orderly thinking, provided by math and science, will prove invaluable to you.

Don't try for an easy escape route by blaming your church and club activities, for that is usually as phony an excuse as the absence-causing ailments at World Series time. The first step on the road up is a change of attitude that comes from putting the blame for the low grades where it belongs. Put away the magnifying glass and get out a mirror. This is *your* job.

2. *Develop good study habits.* Have you ever read 2 Timothy 2:15? It says, "Study to show thyself approved unto God, a workman that needeth not to be ashamed, rightly dividing the word of truth." It refers to your digging into the Bible, but couldn't that first phrase also apply to your high school work? Studying and showing yourself approved seem inevitably to go together.

Many college professors report that one of the biggest problems freshman students face is that of settling down to the kind of study responsibilities that college work requires. A prime cause of failures in the freshman year is that many fellows and girls treat first year college as grade thirteen of high school. High school is the time to develop good study habits.

Here are some tips: (1) Set aside a regular time every day for your studying. Don't let friends, phones, or phonographs interfere. (2) Within the study time, allot earlier and longer periods for your hardest subjects. (3) Study under proper conditions, which means preferably alone in a quiet, well-lighted corner of the house. (4) Get at it! There is nothing in the rule book about an occasional rest period, but make those minutes count.

3. *Keep your daily devotions.* As a young Christian, it is important that you grow spiritually by reading your Bible and having a regular devotional time. It'll help you in your schoolwork, too. You would be amazed at the number of sharp guys and gals

who have told us that getting serious about their Christian life has so changed their outlook on everything that it has helped them pull up their grades too. Drawing closer to the Lord in your own life may give you too a lift in grades that lasts!

Incidentally, I would be much inclined to agree with the high school students who told me on the air that they feel a full day in school is enough and that, other than making up work missed during an absence or voluntarily studying for a test, there should be no homework assignments to be done outside of school hours. These teens feel that six or seven hours a day of studying is enough and that the rest of the day should be free for sports, activities, and work. I concur in that view. But until a majority of educators come around to that position — and I doubt that that will happen overnight — you should do the very best work you are capable of on your assignments.

In the midst of all this material on improving your grades, I want to be fair and realistic. Often too much stress is placed on grades as an end in themselves, instead of on how much is learned. Also, you may have abilities in some subjects and not in others, or your aptitude may not be up to the level of A work at all.

To compare a student not capable of doing superior work to other students who are, is unreasonable and cruel. No one should expect more than your best — whatever it may be. If you are not the most intellectually inclined, you may have other talents and interests you should be developing. You may have great potential for success in those areas.

Then there is the all-important element of the quality of teaching available, a factor over which you have little or no control. Most students have far more interest in their classes when the emphasis is placed on relevance, thinking, and involvement instead of merely memory drill. It's a tragic waste of your talent and enthusiasm to have to memorize facts rather than solve problems or express your interests and ideas, especially when the material being memorized seems irrelevant to your world. Little wonder interest and grades fall behind in such a situation.

The prodding in this chapter has been aimed at the student who has the ability to do better and who because of indifference or poor study habits isn't suffering from overexertion of the brain cells. Fair enough?

With these qualifications, we're aiming at you. Once you've done your preparation and study faithfully, you are in a position to ask the Lord for help, knowing that "He heareth us in whatsoever we ask," and that "if He heareth us, we know that we have the petitions that we desire of Him." During exams, God can bring to your mind things you have studied and read, but not if you have never completed your earlier assignments. Work as though it all depended on you, and pray as though it all depended on God.

This mark-maker method is not copyrighted. So try it and pass it along.

6

The Dating Game

There's no point in telling teens to quit thinking about sex. What most teens are after is sound information so they'll know *how* and *what* to think about sex. Opponents of sex education argue, "You'll just get the kids' curiosity up." You know better. Not only do you have your own thoughts on sex but many of those ideas have been put into practice. When parents won't discuss sex with young people, either because of ignorance or fear, they are only inviting a further barrier to happy family relations. Parents and teens often approach adolescent romance from quite opposite points of view.

Whether it be the first traces of adolescent attraction in junior high school ("He held me close — a cold chill ran down my spine — I thought it was love — but it was just his popsicle melting"!) or promiscuous high schoolers trying to convince each other they're mature by making out and having sexual relations, the question "Is it really love?" looms large in young minds.

Let's begin with a few things both parents and teens can agree love isn't:

Love isn't having a good time. A couple has an out-of-this-world good time on a number of dates and they're sure they're made for each other, for life. But the qualities that make someone fun to be with are not necessarily those that will enable them to be good partners in planning a home and raising a family.

Love isn't sexual attraction. The problem comes up here when petting or intercourse becomes a part of the dating arrangement and are relied upon for satisfaction by the two involved. They confuse sex with the whole person.

Love isn't escaping problems. I know two teen-agers who insist they are deeply in love. Both are high school juniors. Both are unhappy at home and come together to sympathize with each other. Be-cause of their insecurity they rely far too much on each other and are constantly pooling their respec-tive woes. ("If you think that's bad, wait until I tell you what *my* folks did today.") Failure at school, frustration on the job, or seemingly insur-mountable personal problems can all head a teen-ager into a relationship not built on strength and confidence, but on fear and a desire for escape.

A girl may be so starved for some love in her life when she feels unhappy at home that she mistakes a boy's physical desires for the love she craves. Tragically, the boy may not really care for the girl at all and may quickly tire of her, leaving her for some other predatory male to use for his own pur-poses. The girl may go along, trying to convince herself she really is lovable.

The fellow who is frustrated at home may well go

further in his dating relationships than the fellow whose family ties give him a sense of security. The young man who feels unwanted and unappreciated at home will try in every way to gain attention, often confusing this with acceptance, in the hope he will feel loved and wanted. In seeking an emotionally satisfying experience, he settles too quickly for merely physical gratification. Only later does he discover it leaves him disappointed and unsatisfied.

Love isn't material things. He has the sharpest car on campus and a pile of money. She has the most elaborate wardrobe in the group and a neat summer beach home. They were made for each other — or were they?

Love isn't domination. They like each other. Each says nothing can ever come between them. But if he smiles at another girl, she'll sulk for a week. If she chats with another fellow, her steady is on the phone right after school wanting to know what's going on. A mature love seeks to free the other person and protect him in this freedom.

Love isn't glamor. Glamor is all that stuff you read about in the magazines and that you wash off each night. Many a guy fell in love with a vision, only to have her turn into a sight. Beauty goes much deeper — beyond the physical to the inner qualities of life that will last.

Then what is love? Let me dig up a good definition for you:

"Love is very patient and kind, never jealous or envious, never boastful or proud, never haughty or selfish or rude. Love does not demand its own way. It is not irritable or touchy. It does not hold grudges and will hardly even notice when others do it wrong. It is never glad about injustices, but rejoices whenever truth wins out. If you love someone you will be loyal to him no matter what the cost. You will always believe in him, always expect the best of him, and always stand your ground in defending him . . . [That type of love] goes on forever."

Where did that come from? *Seventeen* or *Teen Magazine?* Certainly not from *Playboy!* It's from the Bible (1 Corinthians 13:4-8). Dating is a preparation for love and for the most exciting adventure of this life, marriage. And the love that is at the heart of that relationship needs to be sensible, mature, and real.

What about sexual relations and dating? Frankly, there is probably a lot more talk about loose morals and free love, even at Berkeley, than there is actual practice. A good amount of the talk is done for adult shock effect. Actually many teenagers have rather definite and appropriate limits set for their personal conduct. Some have not, and these young people usually operate on the mistaken assumption that availability sexually is a sure route to popularity, which of course it isn't. It *can* make a girl a popular subject for talk in the boy's locker room; but attention is not respect.

One of the problems is often that boys and girls view dating differently. The boy may be much more casual, with little concern for the girl. He may simply be responding to his biological urge or using the relationship as a prop to his failing ego, a diversion from feelings of inadequacy. Such a boy is apt to get all he can sexually and shrug it off with a flippant, "Why not?"

Often a girl plays at sex, for which she's not ready, because what she wants is love; and a boy plays at love, for which he's not ready, because what he wants is sex.

Some girls foolishly feel that giving in is the key to popularity. They fear if they don't give the guys the gratification they are seeking, they won't be invited out again.

I've counseled many teens on this aspect of their life, and we've discussed it over the radio, my callers remaining anonymous, of course. Here's what I was told: when two people have to sneak around and are afraid of being caught, the relationship is rarely pleasant or rewarding. A girl told me she had thought sneaking off for an all-night make-out session would really be wonderful, but when it was over she said they both felt cheap and degraded.

Certainly the normal attraction of guys and gals for each other is not wrong. There's nothing degrading or immoral about it when used the way it was intended. What determines whether sex is good or bad is whether it is under control.

Sex is like a fire. On a cold night, there is nothing more comfortable and welcome than a warm fire, but that same fire raging out of control can destroy your home and your life. So it is with sex. Within the framework of the marriage relationship, it becomes a beautiful, exhilarating experience; on the sly it turns one of life's most rewarding experiences into a nightmare.

Saving sex for marriage gives you something special to share with the one you marry, something no one else can have. Waiting is so much more satisfying than living on the edge of physical, emotional, and moral disaster. Waiting is also much more realistic than settling for the idea that all moral standards are relative, as if God had repealed the original Ten Commandments and we now have a do-it-yourself plan.

"Making out" goes far beyond sharing affection. It is often a game in which a person sees how far he can go with a partner. Some young people have not decided how far to go. *A young person who waits until the moment of temptation to decide what his standards are, has no standards.*

The big challenge of teen-age life is not to see how close you can get to temptation without getting hurt. There's an ancient proverb on that subject: He that sticketh head in lion's mouth gets breathing interfered with.

That's why unchaperoned moonlight beach parties — or anything else that brings two people very close together and takes them a long way from the eyes of civilization and stills the voice of conscience — are an invitation to disaster. It's also why no smart girl spends an evening at her boy friend's home when she knows his parents are away, and why she will not have him at her home when her parents are gone.

For parties, invite an adult couple as chaperons who are friendly, aware, and unobtrusive.

We opened our radio phone lines one night to ask, "What are some of the things that bug you most about dating?"

Many of the issues we've been discussing in this chapter came up, but so did many others that aren't so major . . . or are they? They certainly were to the teens who asked them. On most of these questions I let other teen callers do the answering and here's what we dealt with:

What is there to do that's different on a date — a change from the old routine? The phones rang in with all sorts of suggestions. I could hardly turn the dials and write fast enough to keep up. Visit the zoo . . . go skating (roller or ice) . . . see an amateur, school, or college play . . . go to a concert . . . canoeing . . . college or pro sports ranked high — basketball, baseball, football, wrestling and swim meets . . . miniature golf . . . go to the beach . . . the mountains or a park. Several callers suggested that teens take on a project they can work at together: volunteers at a hospital, recreation work or handicrafts at a community center, and tutoring younger children were some of the suggestions.

With those suggestions coming thick and fast, we hit another question: *"My parents don't think I'm old enough to have dates on my own; what can I do?"* That's a pretty tough hurdle when young people think they are ready for more privileges than mom and dad are willing to grant. Our callers suggested trying getting the OK for evenings where a group of teens will be together at a church or school function. When these work out well, it should be a natural step for the parents to approve the one-couple date. One important point there was agreement on: there is no set age when a boy or girl is ready to date; it's an individual matter. How should parents decide when to let their son or daughter date? Our callers answered, in the words of one girl, "When a teen-ager shows maturity by the way he handles his day-by-day responsibilities." (The girl who made that comment ended her call by saying, "I sure hope my parents weren't listening tonight; I'll never hear the end of it!") Nobody said it any better.

How about dating older fellows? At the high school level and older, nobody thought a couple of years difference in age between the girl and her date was a problem, but more than a couple of years — or dates between junior high girls and older fellows, even boys in high school — raised some real questions.

"Why does an older guy want to rob the cradle?" a confident sophomore boy commented, throwing the responsibility on the male. Is he desperate? Do girls in his own age group find him unattractive? What's wrong? The implication was definite: something usually is wrong.

What about blind dates? Here our callers were divided between those who had met somebody wonderful this way and those who were, to put it mildly, disappointed.

The key seemed to be knowing something about the fellow (or girl) and his (or her) reputation, and that of the person setting up the date.

The blind date situation to avoid usually opens up with "There's this guy I don't know very much about, but he has a car . . ."

A boy asked, *"If I send a girl flowers on her*

birthday, will she think I'm really serious about her?"

Yes. Our teen audience said flowers should go only to that special girl and on special occasions — her birthday, when she's ill, Christmas.

A subject I've commented on in another chapter came up on the air — *kissing on dates*. Listen in on this telephone-radio exchange with a guy:

"I try to kiss a girl the first time I take her out."

"Then what?" I asked.

"If I get it, I'm a little disappointed. If those kisses are hard to get I think the girl is something special."

You may not agree with his conclusion, but he pressed his claim to be an expert. He modestly assured me he was "the greatest lover in the junior class . . . the kids from my school who are listening all know who I am." Nobody called to dispute his position — or his advice.

There was just a few minutes of air time left and we used them to run through some pet gripes about dating. Included were:

When the boy phones, he's not specific. Girls said, *please* say who is calling, unless you know her well. She may know three guys named Joe, and the answer to "Guess who this is?" could embarrass both of you. And be specific about the night you want her to go out and what you plan to do on the date. She — and her parents — will be grateful.

Call for her at the door. If you're driving don't honk and expect her to come out like a trained walrus at Marine World.

Be nice to her parents. It can be very important

to her, and you, that you get along well with them. You don't need to spend a long time visiting, but some pleasant conversation and particularly some reassurance as to when they can expect their daughter home will score you points all over the place. They may even like you so well they won't notice the length of your hair!

May I pass on a few suggestions to the girls from the fellows who talked with me on another program:

Guys are pretty good critics of makeup, and I've never heard a girl criticized for using too little. The main gripe is, "She's a nice girl, but she wears too much paint for me." The guys have no aversion to makeup used correctly, which means using it to bring out your natural beauty without its being noticeable. Guys just don't seem to appreciate a girl looking like a Halloween pumpkin with the light gone out. The same goes for hairdos resembling an explosion in a mattress factory.

Practical planning about clothes is as important to a girl as good taste. Your parents won't be able to buy you everything you see, so it's important that you learn how to operate from a basic wardrobe. Skirts, sweaters, and blouses that can be changed around frequently are a help. You can then save your party dresses for the really big occasions. With this plan, your wardrobe can be both varied and inexpensive.

Generally speaking, don't seek out boys and suggest they take you out. You can scare a boy off if you move rapidly in his direction. And he'll outrun you because he hates to be caught. He wants to chase you. On the other hand, it's a valuable thing for you to know when to stop running and how to do it gracefully.

You can't avoid all the heartaches in the dating game, and sometimes what promises to be a wonderful relationship may not work out. I once was deeply in love with a girl I hoped to marry — we had much in common, she was beautiful, and I was sure we were made for each other. We planned to get married when she finished her last semester of college, but we ran aground. She wanted a nice home in the suburbs and a husband who worked five days a week on a regular schedule.

There is nothing wrong with those wishes, but that doesn't happen to be the pattern of my life and work with teen-agers. So, with a good deal of regret, we broke up our relationship. It wasn't easy on either of us, believe me, but it was life — and it may well happen to you before you finally settle on the right one for your life's partner.

Let me assure you as I look back to my teen years I wouldn't have missed those first dating days, the ups and downs, the jealousies and heartaches and happiness, for anything. But we should mature in our relationships with the opposite sex.

We usually start with timid, sometimes awkward, steps to dating. We think, "I love me, and I'm going to take good care of me and see I'm properly treated and have a good time."

Then we grow a bit and we meet someone we like even more and we think, "I like you because you like me — we'll get along well together."

Finally, we reach the place when we can say, "I love you, and I'm going to take good care of you and see you're properly treated and safe and that, no matter what happens to me, all is well with you forever."

I've just received a letter from a young fellow who is student body president of his high school. Both he and his girl friend, close friends of mine, attended a Campus Life leadership conference that was deeply meaningful to both of them. He's permitted me to share some of his letter with you:

"After the Friday night meeting, we had a chance to be alone. It was snowing that night, and it was just beautiful. The whole conference had given me much to think about. So I went out on the lawn in the snow and got on my knees and prayed. I heard someone walking behind me. I looked up and it was Sue. She got down on her knees beside me and prayed with me. I love her very much. It's so wonderful because God is right in the middle of everything we do. God has been very good to both of us, and I'm continually thanking Him for it. I just wanted to get across to you the relationship Sue and I have for one another, filled with God's love for us and our love for Him. Love is great, Gordy, and it is just great to be able to love Sue as a young woman, as beautiful as she is, and to be able to love her through Christ who loves us both."

Strange as it may seem, when we forget ourselves, when we put someone else in first place, we become winners. And that's what love is.

7

HeɾE GomES the JudgE

A highlight of the year at most high schools is the annual awards assembly when students are recognized for outstanding achievements in studies, athletics, leadership, music, drama, and art.

At Mike's school, and for him personally, it was a big day. He was to receive several honors — one for drama, one for music, and another for all-around leadership. This last was a special recognition that included a large scholarship presented by a local civic group.

Mike was a popular student on campus, both with the administration and the student body. His honors were greeted by enthusiastic applause from the students and followed by a nice story and two-column picture in the press. That Monday he was on top of the world.

By Thursday it had all changed. He was in a juvenile detention cell and his confused parents were joined by friends and teachers in asking, "How could it happen to Mike?"

I was no less surprised when a police officer called my office and asked if I knew Mike. Of course I did — anybody close to high school students in the community knew him and liked him. "Well, Mr. McLean, why don't you come down and see him. We've got him locked up."

"You must be kidding," I replied, thinking I was being dragged into some graduation prank. But this was no joke, and one look at Mike across the counseling desk in juvenile hall quickly confirmed it.

For Mike, who was a great public speaker, the life of the party, and a happy extrovert, the words now came haltingly. Tears were in his eyes as he spoke. "I was picked up last night with another guy — we were using drugs — speed [methedrine, a stimulant usually taken by injection] — we had that and some pot in the car and on us when we were stopped — then I was brought here. Jack [the other boy] was older, so they put him in the county jail, and he got bailed out."

Mike's involvement with drugs would take him to court, hurt his family, embarrass his school, and cost him a college scholarship.

How had it all started? Nothing really big — just a few joints at a party a few months back. Everybody was trying it, so Mike went along. It really didn't do much for him; marijuana rarely does. Even trying more later didn't give him any groovy sensations or unusual insights.

But now the guys who were selling the lids [an ounce of marijuana in a plastic wrapper] were also offering something else that was "bigger, better, gives a real flash." It was "speed." The first time he injected he was a little hesitant about the whole idea, but he got a fast flash, enjoyed the experience, and was soon looking for more.

Mike's parents didn't know; he even managed to keep it from his girl friend, a vivacious, beautiful girl, but too "straight" to appreciate his adventures in the world of drugs. If he had kept at it much longer, they probably would have suspected it. A prolonged contact with drugs, even marijuana, usually brings about a carelessness in appearance, a disinterest in studies and activities, and a blasé attitude about life in general.

Mike wasn't hooked. He didn't have a physical need to take drugs as happens with the harder narcotics, but his psychological dependence upon them was increasing. He wanted "speed" and was quite restless and irritable when he didn't have any. He had saved up some money from a summer job on which he could draw, so hadn't had to steal or furnish other students with drugs to get his own supply — yet.

Mike knew his parents would be disappointed and angry; he couldn't blame them. They hadn't yet been down to see him, and he wasn't really looking forward to the meeting with them the next morning.

Mike had had a birthday earlier in that eventful week, on Tuesday. He was now at an age where his case could be transferred for trial to regular adult court. I knew the people who would now be working with Mike — the court officials, investigators, probation staff, attorneys, and judge. I see these people in my daily work with the juvenile court, and it's the story of this work that is told in my book *We're Holding Your Son*.

All of us worked together over the next few weeks in preparation for the court hearing. Like most juvenile courts, this one was interested in helping a young person straighten out, not merely in punishing him. A sincere effort was made to balance kindness with firmness, correction with understanding. The investigator's report prepared to guide the judge brought out Mike's good points as well as his drug problem. His attorney asked the juvenile court to retain jurisdiction in the case and allow Mike to return home on probation.

The judge was interested in what Mike had to say: "I've done some real thinking while I've been here at juvenile hall," — and he had. He loved his parents and was ashamed of hurting them. He and I talked together about the emptiness in a busy life, the weakness in the face of temptation, and the One who could head a young person in a whole new direction when He was at the center of our living. Mike had been to church enough to know the basic facts, but he had been much too busy to stop and look inside until he was suddenly forced to face up to himself. When he did, he didn't like what he saw. Only then was he ready to look to God. Sincerity is hard to measure in a courtroom, but teens can — and do — change, and the phonies are actually a distinct minority.

"It's what you do from this point on that really counts," the judge told Mike. "Today is the first day of the rest of your life." Mike got his break and is now doing well, several years later. He's in college, still a leader — but with a new sense of values and purpose in his life.

Mike's not the only one. There's Jeff, who brought some drugs to school to sell, only to have two girls who made purchases become seriously ill. Because of the selling and near-tragic results, Jeff was sent to the local juvenile rehabilitation facility — a boys' ranch which offers a wide range of good opportunities for rechanneling a young man's life when he wants help. Jeff not only benefited from the ranch program, but from his commitment to the Lord. He has finished high school, is looking forward to a career in business, and is still active in Christian service.

Bob, Jeff's close buddy at that same ranch, was a boy who had everything going for him materially. He was from a home offering him many advantages. Bob didn't appreciate what he had. He ran with a fast crowd, wouldn't listen to authorities, had problems at school, ended up in juvenile court several times, and finally was sent to the county ranch. The counselors know how to relate to boys; and when Bob was ready to listen, they were there to help. He, too, had neglected the spiritual dimension of his life until he realized that the God who made addition tables can beat anybody in the world at adding. Bob came to know the Lord, and his faith became an enthusiastic and dynamic influence in his life. Bob has been home for many months now and is one of the active leaders in our Campus Life program.

Dan, not the young man who wrote the introduction to this book, was at the same juvenile facility.

HOW TO RAISE YOUR PARENTS

He was a young Mexican-American, familiar with the rough and seamy side of life, and the leader of a group of street rebels. He was brilliant, and underneath the belligerent facade, he was anxiously trying to find meaning and purpose for his life. The ranch staff was patient, waiting for him to settle into the program, to take his schooling seriously, and to begin to lower his barriers of suspicion. When he was ready, they began to build on the foundation of trust that had been laid. Dan and I got acquainted, and I pointed him to the One who could take eager, young enthusiasm and build it into a worthwhile life. Today Dan is back in the community and still a leader — only now it's on the right side.

Sometimes a guy has to learn the hard way that his parents are right, that going along with something in order to be one of the boys or because the crowd is doing it, can lead to tragedy. For Rick, the results were just that. He was a senior in high school but looked older. He didn't see why he shouldn't drink when he could pass for the legal age. He was even "kind" enough to get some extra booze for some of the younger high school fellows.

One night Rick supplied three fellows with a case of beer for a Friday night party and didn't give the incident a second thought. After downing much of the booze they went out riding in a stolen car, picking up a fourth boy to join them. There was a deserted area at the edge of town which they considered ideal for testing their speed and driving skills, as well as their ability to hold their liquor. That's where they headed.

They drove back and forth picking up speed and daring as their spirits soared. They missed one turn and crashed into a tree, throwing three of the boys out of the car, but leaving their fourth passenger, Bob, age fifteen, bleeding and dying in the car. The boys panicked and simply left — leaving Bob to die.

After the three boys were apprehended, the court was interested in the source of their illegal supply of alcohol. Furnishing alcohol to minors is a serious charge; and when that offense results in death, the charge is manslaughter.

Rick — whom I came to know very well — was crushed, and what the court could do to him was almost incidental to the grief and heartbreak he will carry all his life. Bob — the boy who died — was Rick's brother.

Of course, this case is unusually severe; but it is true. Alcohol can get a teen-ager into trouble — bad trouble.

Fortunately, getting into trouble has been the real turning point in the lives of many teens. However, the fact that experience is a good teacher doesn't make it the best, or only, teacher. Please don't learn the hard way. *When you play loose, you play to lose.*

A student asked high school assembly speaker Don Lonie what makes the difference in teen-agers, and Don replied, "The three R's: responsibility, respect, and religion." There it is in a nutshell.

Responsibility — You want to be treated like an adult, but do you act like one? Can your word be trusted? Do you follow through with a job or with your studies?

Respect — Do you think enough of your parents and yourself not to do something foolish just because a certain crowd think it's "in"?

Religion — Do you just give God one hour a week, if that much? Or is the One who gave His life for you in control of yours?

What's all this stuff about courts and law doing in this book anyway? It's here because 52 percent of all crimes committed in America are committed by young people aged thirteen to seventeen. It's here because drug arrests of teen-agers in the state of California, for one, rose 2000 percent in the last eight years. It's here because one out of four teens in this country will be dealt with by the law for something more serious than a traffic violation. It's here because the breakdown in parent-teen relationships often results in a frustrated teen getting in more trouble than he ever imagined when he decided to run away, drop out, get even, or fight back.

It's *not* here because I think all teens are uncaught juvenile delinquents, although many a sharp guy or gal who didn't think, or got careless, or went along with a crowd, or thought just once wouldn't hurt found out they were wrong. It's *not* here because I'm down on teens who get into trouble with the law. I spend a great deal of my time helping them, and I include many of them among my closest friends. But speaking for all of us who have any connection with juvenile court, we're not looking for business!

More than two thousand young people a month

come to the Free Clinic in Los Angeles where a staff of sociologists, physicians, teachers, psychologists, dentists, and a growing number of young people who originally came for help and are now helpers, team up to lend assistance to teens involved with drug abuse.

Dr. Barry Liebowitz, a volunteer on the staff, states, "I think these kids have gone to the spiritual values first. They say, 'Let me find out what I really believe in and get some tranquility within myself, and then I'll decide how to earn a living.' And so there's no dialogue between us and them. Many parents don't pay any attention to what their young folks say, so the young folks decide they may as well leave home to see if they can get a chance to talk and find some friends."

A unique approach to educating parents on the drug abuse problem is a Los Angeles program called DARE, Drug Abuse Research and Education, a presentation to adults by teen-agers themselves with the counsel of one of the nation's top authorities on drugs, Dr. Thomas Ungerleider, of the U.C.L.A. Neuropsychiatric Institute. These young people, who look for all the world like drug users are imagined to look, carefully explain drug effects, terminology, and the causes of parent-teen communication breakdowns to interested audiences. None of these young people use drugs, and when asked why they reply, "We don't have to — we're turned on to life!"

If you're interested in various laws and court procedures as they relate specifically to teen-agers, be sure to read *Teen-agers and the Law,* written by John Paul Hanna, an attorney.

A unique approach to acquainting teen-agers with the law has been taken by some high schools in Harrisburg, Pennsylvania. Each Tuesday local attorneys give their time to instruct voluntary classes on laws that affect young people. Student response has been great and was pretty well summarized by a tenth grader's comment to *Parade* magazine. "It has made me more aware of the two sides of the law — one side tells me I *can't* do certain things, but the other guarantees that I *can* do certain things."

You might also enjoy reading of my experiences during my many years of working with teen-agers in trouble with the law. They are in my book entitled *We're Holding Your Son.*

I wish you could meet the many young people whose stories I've told in that book. The young man who wrote the foreword to the book was tragically involved in the drug scene. He and another young man were charged with second degree murder after his girl friend died from an overdose of cocaine.

I met Drew shortly after his arrest and spent many hours with him after he was released on bail. He was anxious both to reorient his life away from drugs and to find some better answer to the psychological hang-ups that had caused him to use narcotics extensively. It was no easy battle, but eventually Drew made a commitment of his life to the Lord which was the major step in his building a new life.

He became deeply concerned about the increasing number of high school students, just a few years younger than he, who were starting out on drugs. He agreed to join me in a series of drug abuse education programs on campus. He enjoyed talking with students, but did not particularly appreciate having to relive the details of a tragedy in front of thousands of students, nor he was unmindful of the potential jeopardy at his trial from the frank answers he was giving to students' questions.

The program was most effective. Students listened to Drew because he was young, and they had read about the tragedy in which he was involved. The newspapers gave good publicity to the school programs, and our schedule was full until a court order was issued, stopping all pretrial statements that might prejudice a fair trial. The charges against Drew were lowered by the court to involuntary manslaughter, and both young men entered guilty pleas to the reduced charge. Drew was confined to the county jail, a facility that offers both a work furlough and college release program, for eight months; his companion was sent to a state youth institution for an indefinite period.

In the assemblies many students asked Drew about marijuana, which some of them thought was harmless and ought to be legalized. Drew did not agree, and indicated he doubted marijuana would ever be legalized for teen-agers. He pointed out that marijuana, while not physically addictive, can produce a disinterest in studies, sports, and other worthwhile pursuits and often produces a psychological dependence which can be harder to break than physical addiction. While not everyone who uses marijuana goes on to heavier drug involvement, Drew pointed out that all his circle of friends who had started with "grass" were now either heavy drug users or in jail — and one was in a mental hospital.

What about the generation gap as a causal factor in drug use? Drew didn't think so. He felt the phrase was often used by teens themselves to evade parents and by parents to avoid having to relate meaningfully to their own teenagers.

Students also asked about other drugs — LSD, "speed," "reds" (seconal tablets, a barbiturate) and THC. THC is an increasingly popular synthetic form of marijuana first developed by Dr. Edward Taylor and a Princeton research team. The United States Army is interested in its use to incapacitate an enemy by reducing his will to reason, to concentrate, and to coordinate. Obviously it does the same things to youthful experimenters.

Drew, who plans to enter the ministry and specialize in youth counseling after completing his education, helped many young people. But no program will prove effective with all students. Teen drug abuse — and other problems — continue to plague many teens. This week I've seen

— a high school athlete with a previously clean record picked up for smoking pot.

— a high school pusher busy selling "reds" until one of his trusted customers turned out to be a narc (police narcotics agent).

— a junior who rebelled, left home, and set up business selling drugs at an obliging neighbor boy's home until a police raid terminated his thriving venture.

— a young girl from a broken home whose mother is an alcoholic; the girl is now in custody for shoplifting.

— a high school sophomore who was so impatient to drive, he "borrowed" a neighbor's car only to find that joyriding may not be the biggest crime in the world, but it will do for a start.

— an eighth grader who thought he was a big man because he sniffed glue.

— a boy who stole *my* Dodge Charger and later was involved in an accident.

I assure you I'll do everything I can to help each of these fellows and girls get their lives straightened out and on the right track. So will many other people. But if you have ideas like theirs, or anything close to them, do yourself and your parents a big favor — forget it.

8

You, your parents, and your Future

Be a success.

That's the goal, isn't it? Your parents have had it in the back of their minds since day one as they plotted your future. The school counselors have all been telling you how important it is to work up to your ability so you can get into the right college or land the right job. You've probably long since caught the signals indicating that the right career can get you all the good things in life.

In our society, success is most often measured in terms of material things — nice home, two cars, color television set, boat, beach place, expensive wardrobe. There's nothing wrong with wanting or enjoying these things. I can't find anywhere that God made poverty a virtue; besides, it can be ridiculously inconvenient.

My question is: are material things success in themselves, or a by-product, in some cases, of success? I know too many people who have everything money can buy but know little of a happy home, an untroubled mind, or a good night's sleep. The eight-million-plus alcoholics in America are a tragic testimonial to the effects of pressure-cooker living on insecure people. And if a man has to take pep pills to get up, take a tranquilizer to relax, visit his psychiatrist to unbend, and take a barbiturate to sleep, what real value is there in each day's routine?

The problem is not that the average American has nice things, but that nice things have the average American. Instead of enjoying the luxuries he can take for granted (many things people across the world have never even dreamed of) he has become a slave to them. He holds down two jobs and his wife works — not for necessities, but more often to make the monthly payments on their luxuries.

It happens on the teen level, too. Joe has a nice car. Why? Because he has to drive to work, naturally. And why does he have to work? To support the car! There's nothing wrong with Joe's working or having his car. But if an auto is all he has to show for his efforts, if he has let his studies and other obligations go by the board while he works to keep that car going, something is out of kilter. He may well be the type who will grow up to have the nicest things — and neither the time, energy, or health to enjoy them.

If success isn't how much you make or how much you have, then what is it? The best definition of success I've run across is this: *Success is finding out what God wants you to do, and doing it!*

As long as we're not just biological accidents we ought to consider Who put us here, and why. If that guide for the future sounds a little way out, consider the alternatives:

1. You can pick a career by accident. Maybe you know somebody who heard about an opening, took the job, and has been at it ever since — same old routine, not much chance for advancement. He's in a rut — which is a grave with the ends knocked out.

2. You can follow in your father's footsteps — which is all right only if that career is best for you. The decision is yours.

3. You can put your I.Q., grade point average, interests, and aptitudes into the nearest computer,

push the buttons, and let the machine tell you what you're best suited for vocationally. (If it says ballerina and you're a rugged football player, you'd better start over.)

There is another route. You can take an honest look at your strengths and weaknesses, attitudes and interests, resources and opportunities, then you can talk with some people whose judgment you respect, and in it all ask God for His direction which He has promised when we honestly seek it.

"If you want favor with God and man, and a reputation for good judgment and common sense, then trust the Lord completely; don't ever trust yourself. In everything you do, put God first; and He will direct you and crown your efforts with success" (Prov. 3:4-6).

In Psalm 1, David outlines a pattern for success that follows right along the same lines:

"Happy is the man who walks not in the counsel of the ungodly." *Get your advice from the right people.*

"Delight in . . . and desire the law of the Lord." *Get your pleasures from the right things.*

". . . Nor sits down with scorners and mockers." *Get your friends from the right source.*

What does David conclude about a man who follows those directions? "Everything he does shall prosper and come to maturity."

Let's take a look at that first point again — where your advice comes from. Many people can and should help. Don't be afraid to ask them. Begin with your parents. Learn from what they tell you and what you've observed, both good and bad.

Be sure to include your pastor or church youth director. Here are dedicated people trained in giving sound spiritual counsel.

Talk with a counselor at school — certainly this is a must in filling out college applications and gathering admissions data. But I have a note of warning: some school counselors tend to promote certain schools to which they are partial, and not all of these counselors fully appreciate the desire of a young person to attend a Christian college for a particular type of education. Further, the position of a school counselor can tend, at times, to make their word almost law. This is a position you cannot allow them to take. Remember it's *your* life, *your* convictions, and *your* future.

Should you go to college? That has to be your choice, but there is no doubt it will open doors to many opportunities and services you will never have without a degree. If you have a chance to get more education, by all means do so.

What about getting into a good college? Here are some of the facts:

1. *Good high school grades are important,* but many colleges rely heavily on the College Entrance Examination Board tests and the grade prediction tests. If you've been a little slow at taking your high school work seriously, this will give you a chance to show your college admissions officer you are capable of doing the work.

2. *Carefully study the catalog of the college you hope to attend.* It will point out particular areas the school emphasizes and in which you have abilities — art, music, journalism, athletics — and you

can stress those specialties in your application. You might even apply for a scholarship.

3. *Consider geography.* Some schools make a special effort to see they have a broad geographic representation in their student body, and this may help you gain admission to a college in another section of the country.

4. *Watch deadlines.* Get your application in early, and both your chances and your choices will be better.

The federal government has a number of loan programs designed to help you with your education should you need them. Your school counselor can give you information, or you can write to the Division of Student Financial Aid, U.S. Office of Education, Washington, D.C.

In a nuclear age when mankind could be reduced to an ash in a flash and where our globe has shrunk to the point where a crisis anywhere becomes a threat to all of us, a young man has to consider his military obligation.

There is much talk about changing the draft laws. The new lottery system is already in effect, and President Nixon and others have urged that an all-volunteer army of well-paid professional soldiers take the place of the draft.

Some fellows go into the service because they're bored with school, hard up for a job, or unhappy at home. It really doesn't make much sense to join the service to run away from something. Three or four years is a long time to run, and you may return home frustrated to find all your friends much further along with their education or careers.

On the other hand, if you want the specialized training the Air Force, Navy, and Army schools can provide, joining the service might well be the wisest move you've ever made. You can fulfill your military obligation and at the same time learn some valuable skills that will allow you many opportunities for advancement in civilian life.

For a young person who hasn't traveled much, life in the service can appear to be an ideal existence. A visit to a basic training camp can quickly dispel those ideas. Moving from place to place has its fun and challenges, but there are also plenty of disappointments and frustrations.

If you're interested, talk to a recruiter, but with this note of caution. These men are not above stretching a point in their own favor, though most of them will try to give you honest and sound counsel. Realize, too, the service is interested primarily in what you can do for them, not the other way around. That's why many volunteers and draftees feel they're not always getting the best deal. But that can happen with any job.

You're considering a job, more education, or the service. Where does God's will fit into all this?

Doesn't a young person have to be a missionary, pastor, or nurse to be doing the Lord's work? Not necessarily. For a Christian, there is no difference between secular and sacred. All ground is holy ground. We're never "off duty." That means God can call a young person to be a teacher, a company executive, an accountant, an estate planner, a contractor, a power products salesman, a housewife, a nurse, or a beautician just as much as He can call a man to the pulpit.

In fact, there are some people in the ministry who were pressured into it by well-meaning friends and circumstances who could be much happier — and more effective as Christians — working in the business world.

I've been in a specialized ministry to youth all of my adult life and I really wouldn't want to do anything else. The hours are long, the pay is low, and there are disappointments, frustrations, and more than enough people coming along to criticize to keep me reasonably humble. But it's all worth it. When you see young people whose lives will never be the same again because they've met the Lord, you sense the thrill and excitement of working with youth. It's just the greatest. But it's not for everybody, and it may not be for you.

My advice to young people asking about any phase of the ministry for their life's work is this: If you can be happy doing anything else, then by all means do it; but if nothing else in the whole world is so important to you as sharing your faith in the Lord with no distractions, then come on! We need you.

In the final analysis, there are three decisions that go into making a young person's life a success. Make these three right, and you've got it. Miss the boat on them, and I don't care how rich, intelligent, or famous you become — you won't know what success really is.

1. *Accept Christ as your personal Savior.* Don't

just go to church, but invite Him into the very center of your mind, your will, your emotions.

2. *Take your hands off your own life and let the Lord run it.* . . . the God who made you has a perfect plan for your life; let Him guide you into it.

3. *Pick the right life partner.* It takes three to make a marriage: a young couple deeply in love and Christ as the Lord of their home. Please! Don't "fall" in love. Wedding bells and your love life will determine a lot of your future — which is the key here. In fact, it's all-important that you not fall in love. The idea is, "Don't fall into love — grow into love." We're not just playing with words! The popular American myth is to fall in love, and that is a dangerous idea. Sure, emotions should play a large part. But the brain had better be in gear as well. Some girls actually dislike their guys, but still plan to marry them because they "fell" in love and are all emotionally wrapped around the finger. Well, they'll fall all right — into a second-rate life, and possibly divorce.

You can face the future with confidence. To what I have just suggested the editors of *Campus Life* magazine add these very practical suggestions.

1. *Grow like a human being,* not like an orange crate. Orange crates don't grow. They stay the same shape, size, and strength. Some people are like that. They're old men or women at seventeen. They figure few people can teach them anything. Such adages as "The mark of genius is to be astonished, not to astonish" and "There are more things in heaven and earth than your philosophy has ever dreamed of" go sailing right over their heads. You

will either grow in the next few years — or you'll stagnate and become a pool of fears and frustrations.

2. *Lock in tight!* Frankly, if we had to face the surging 1970s alone, we'd feel like copping out. It's almost impossible to be an idealist about where man is going, and where society is taking us. No matter how exciting the medicines and moon shots and new products, prejudice and racism and ordinary pettiness all around us overshadow the "bright future." Despair grips earthlings when they think of really doing anything about the vast problems of the human race.

3. *Open up.* Now, you can't do this unless you "lock in," because it's unnerving at times, listening to opposing viewpoints and having to reevaluate your own. It can be demoralizing, this trying to understand people who are different from you, whose ideas seem foreign, even dangerous. It's tough to accept everybody as humans to love.

Sure, you could close your mind like a clam and live in your world where everyone agrees with you. But growth, and love, and relationships in our tension-filled world mean seeing all human beings as objects of love — particularly unlovable humans.

4. *Expect ashes in your mouth* or, don't deify the "now" generation. Are you developing maturity? Enough to roll with the punch when your leader — the one you most respect — really blows it? Or when you get excited about people with great ideas for a new life style, and they eventually prove themselves pretty hollow? During the next ten years, you'll probably taste some ashes. Don't let it floor you.

5. *Discover the unique you.* Chances are you feel inferior about something. Most teen-agers stepping the 1970s do, and you're probably no exception. Looks, brains, family background, whatever — you probably feel you've been shortchanged. "God, grant me the serenity to accept things I cannot change, courage to change things I can, and wisdom to know the difference." This applies to your personality as well as to externals. You want to grow, correct weaknesses, get over bad habits.

6. *Burn your labeling machine.* This makes beautiful relationships with others possible. Many want to relate only to people who agree with them and to make up labels for everybody else. It's the great old labels game. You play it. Your parents play it. We all play it. Put a name on the forehead of a person so we can write him off as a human being. It's a tragic pastime.

7. *Grab onto "high-octane, quality living."* No matter how many changes flash around you, the quality of your living doesn't have to shrivel. Not if you're putting your face into the winds of challenge and digging your feet into something solid and secure.

9

Civil
Disobedience

If there is any issue that sets the younger generation and their parents at odds, it is the current wave of campus unrest and youthful protest. Strong feelings prevail on both sides, and emotions run high.

You may be able to confine your interest to classroom and home discussions while you're still in high school, but once on a college campus, you will instantly be faced with some very vital choices that will leave you on the sidelines or propel you to the center of the action.

You should realize the basis for your parents' concern. When your dad was younger, he did as he was told. The idea of students insisting on a voice in running a school was about the last thing he could imagine. And as for a bunch of radicals blocking a military induction center, he knew what to do there too — put them through basic training and ship them to the hottest part of the war.

Your generation for the most part thinks differently. Many of you feel that if someone believes a particular war is wrong, he has an obligation to do everything he can to oppose it, including violating the law.

There is quite a change in our thoughts about patriotism. Some have suggested we do away with the pledge of allegiance to the flag and the national anthem at public events, and many consider national pride an evil hangover from a bygone era that actually puts barriers between people. At the opposite extreme, patriotism is defined in such narrow terms that a citizen who questions any act of government is suspected of disloyalty.

In the past, if a young person was indifferent to

then-current standards, he still showed some respect for the forces of law. The policeman and the man in the military were looked up to, and their uniform was a point of pride. Today the sight of a uniform too often invites scorn and crude disrespect.

John Fischer, former editor of *Harper's Magazine,* recently listed four choices young people today have. The choices: drop out, flee, plot a revolution, or try to change the world gradually, one clod at a time.

To a young person who takes his spiritual commitment seriously, the present upheaval can present major problems. How should he react to those who show contempt for their nation on the grounds that to be true to God they must challenge their country when they believe it is wrong? It's all more than just a bit confusing to a teen trying to be true to himself and his own conscience, as well as to his parents and their values. May I make a few suggestions in this and the next chapter.

Christians have a responsibility to be good citizens and actively participate in the governing of their land. Bad men get elected when good men won't run. Certainly an individual can fulfill God's plan for his life in government service just as in any other occupation. But what if the government of a nation is evil?

The Word of God gives us some straight counsel: "Obey the government, for God is the one who put it there. There is no government anywhere that God has not placed in power. So those who refuse to obey the laws of the land are refusing to obey

God, and punishment will follow" (Romans 13:1, 2).

Peter also wrote, "For the Lord's sake, obey every law of your government: those of the king as head of state, and those of the king's officers, for he has sent them to punish all who do wrong, and to honor those who do right" (1 Peter 2:13, 14).

I do not believe, however, that we are to follow every government order, no matter what that order says. If the government should require something contrary to God's Word, the Christian cannot, and must not, obey that order. The Bible's teaching is that governments get their authority from God and that men should obey God's word in cases of conflict. This is why Peter, when ordered to stop preaching the Gospel, bluntly refused, saying, "We must obey God rather than men" (Acts 5:29).

The difficulty comes in determining *when* disobedience to the rules of men is necessary in order to do God's will. Let there be no hesitation: if the laws of nations are contrary to God's will, it is God who must be obeyed.

When told to quit proclaiming the good news of Christ or face the consequences, the early Christians by the thousands chose imprisonment and martyrdom. It is reasonable to assume there were some who counseled that it might be better to water down the message and get along with the rulers of the day; but there is no evidence many took that route. Their convictions were neither for sale nor subject to compromise.

The issues are not always so clear-cut today. Scriptural quotations are used to justify every conceivable political and social position, and in some circles people talk as though God were a registered member of a certain political party. People will misuse the Bible to "prove" that income tax is wrong, that blacks are an inferior race, that capital punishment is good, and that any economic system other than laissez-faire capitalism is anti-God. It takes some doing to distort Scripture that way, but it is done. Somewhere en route emotion and human opinion take over from reason and spiritual maturity.

Curran Tiffany, a Washington, D.C. attorney active in the program of Young Life, comments in *Focus on Youth*. "Though Christ may be truthfully characterized as revolutionary in his earthly ministry, he did not attack or even criticize the rotten political and social system; he excoriated only those who professed to speak for God or who profaned God's house . . . It is good to challenge every Christian with the needs one sees. But as the Bible says, 'Judge not.' We cannot condemn other Christians who we believe are not as socially enlightened or active in some area as we are."

About now you might rightly conclude the Bible is going to offer very little encouragement for those who are looking for God's approval on overthrowing their government by unlawful means, whether in a free or captive state. One thing is sure — it becomes risky business to try and make Scripture fit your theories; it works much better in reverse.

Does this leave the concerned believer sitting idly on the sidelines while all sorts of problems and challenges confront our society? I don't think so!

If governments find their source in God, then it must be our duty as God's children to do everything we can to make them strong and just. It is not only our privilege, but our duty. A Christian has an obligation to work at being a good citizen.

How can you as a teen-ager meet that obligation?

1. Keep informed on the issues and leaders that affect your campus, your community, and your nation.

2. Consider becoming an active politician. Politics is only evil when people let it become so. Join a club, work for a candidate, contribute money and time. In recent years, the student world has revolutionized the political world and brought a much-needed breath of fresh air to the traditionally smoke-filled rooms of the professional vote getters.

3. Work on problems with others who are seeking positive solutions. Help in a ghetto school, work in a voter registration drive, attend community meetings and express your views, and push to have the voting age lowered.

There are lots of challenges in this country and many things that need changing. Thank God we live in a country that can and does change — not always as fast as we'd like — but it does change.

Where the Christian encounters a clear violation of the principles of God's Word, he *must* disobey, and not gripe at facing the consequences of his action. But where things are wrong by human standards, he is obligated to work through the channels of his government for the changes he deems necessary, giving that government the obedience he owes it as a child of God. To break the law in order to change a law you think is bad is not justified — even if the man urging you to do so is a distinguished professor with as many degrees as a sauna bath. Education should lead to wisdom, but it doesn't always — some men die by degrees. While you can be young only once, many people manage to be immature for a long time.

All of these opinions may lead to misunderstandings between parents and students, requiring a great deal of patience and tact if the lines of communication are to remain open when the "status quo" collides with your "let's go."

10

"I Want to Get Involved!"

Free speech!
The New Morality!
Social revolution!
Overthrow! Violence! Defiance!

These are the watchwords of visionaries on campuses around the world. Join a march, sign a petition, start a protest, grow a beard, chant a slogan. Or if these activities don't appeal, go the opposite route — protest the protesters.

Students are obviously doing much more than simply studying contemporary problems in classrooms or discussing them in dormitory bull sessions. More often than not, they are coming to grips with the issues of the day — dramatically and forcefully. There is no shortage of leadership for any brand of student enthusiasm. The heroes of the left have become the Staughton Lynds and Thomas Haydens. The rightists draw inspiration from the William Buckleys and Robert Welchs. The black activists follow in the steps of Stokely Carmichael and Eldridge Cleaver.

None of this activity is any too comforting to parents who are almost invariably a great deal more conservative than their offspring and wonder just what effect campus exposure will have on a son or daughter.

Throughout these protest dramas, religion has been highly abused and warped. God becomes just another tool. His blessing has been invoked on a weird assortment of fanatics on both sides of every fence. Religion has also served as a convenient escape hatch for those who, wishing to remove themselves from the unpleasantness of the contemporary scene, have become spiritual mystics and political hermits.

There is little doubt the majority of young, daring intellectuals out to remake our world have long since written off religion in general and Christianity in particular. To them, both are irrelevant and meaningless.

The fault is not all theirs. The blasé attitude of the average student has undoubtedly been spawned by modern churchmen who have managed to imprison Christ in stained-glass windows, uninspiring rituals, meaningless recitation, and abundant negatives. Even religious leaders of our day think so little of the Savior that they often give greater credence to the newest theological fads than they do to His teachings and may even announce that God is dead. The typical student's attitude says, "The church itself doesn't know what it believes any longer. Why then should I be concerned with God, Christ, or morality?" No wonder he is skeptical, cynical, or simply bored when he sees the insipid, paltry efforts masquerading as spiritual dedication in much of contemporary church life.

That Jesus Christ Himself has often paled into insignificance behind artificial facades is tragic. If religion's verbal portraits of Jesus leave much to be desired, the artists have only added to the degradation. The more familiar portraits of the Galilean are quite unappealing. Christ is drawn as a weak, mild, emaciated individual desperately in need of some vitamins, if not Geritol! It is not hard to see how a man thus portrayed, and considered only as a historical figure long since dead, could be ignored by a tuned-in generation.

What a far cry all this is from the authentic description of Christ provided in the Bible! He was so much more than a complacent theorist — Jesus Christ was, in fact, the greatest revolutionary history has ever known. Take a good look.

He was a real man. Carpentry was His trade, and fishermen were His closest friends. He lived all of His life in the outdoors. He was an outcast rejected by both the establishment of His day and His own people. He upset those at ease by demanding nothing less than a complete about-face in their living patterns — selfishness, greed, and immorality were to be replaced by concern, generosity, and love. His sternest rebukes were given to those who cloaked themselves in formal religion and phony piety.

He was not content to deal with surface symptoms. Jesus Christ seized root causes. He was not afraid to "tell it like it is!" He declared that man's basic problems do not stem from his color, his environment, or his educational inadequacies. The trouble with man, He declared, was a corrupt innate

101

nature. The solutions He prescribed go beyond psychotherapy, a better standard of living, or a higher culture. He declared that every area of a man's being — physical, mental, social, and spiritual — needs transformation. And this transformation is possible only when a man opens the doors of motive, intellect, and will to Christ.

The people of His day were disappointed. He did not fit the accepted pattern, nor say the things they wanted to hear. If only He had led a revolution against the party in power and become a governmental ruler! Was not this the way to solve problems?

But no! He demanded men be changed — and then transformed men could make their influence felt in every area of society. In fact, men who truly followed Him could do no less than meaningfully affect the world around them.

Even in His rejection, Christ promised victory. It was here that He raised the tallest, most significant placard of history. He conquered man's greatest enemy, death, by walking out of a tomb in triumph and leaving the grave an empty shell. He told His followers that some day they would do the same things; and if death could be conquered, what power on earth was there to fear?

It's easy to be a modern skeptic. All you have to do is laugh at the divine, scorn the devout, and slur the sacred. Perhaps we should recall that only two groups found Christ as a baby in the manger: the shepherds and the wise men — the simple and the learned — those who knew that they knew nothing and those who knew they did not know everything.

It's not hard to be a reactionary. Live in the past. Assume all was good way back when. Fight all changes. Denounce all who disagree with you as disloyal or duped. Insist we turn back the clock. Never come to grips with issues. Don't get involved except to oppose.

It's also quite simple to be a radical. Demand changes and insist all change is progress. Talk about freedom, but never mention responsibility. Defy authority, look like a slob, shout vulgarities, feed your mind on obscenities, call purity abnormal, let your thinking be done in Moscow or Peking, conform to the rest of the hippies while telling everybody you're a nonconformist.

But what kind of a person does it take to be a friend of Jesus Christ? It requires one who is not swayed by the passions of the moment, nor led down blind trails by the pseudo-intellectual, one who is not content with the nominally religious or the politely pious, one unwilling to be detoured by the materially profitable or the morally degrading, one who is kind and understanding when insulted and misunderstood. The friend of Christ is a willing servant of all men, but a slave to none, sometimes denying legitimate pleasures in order to better crucify egotism. He is prepared to die for his faith and yet is involved in doing something much more demanding — living it day by day.

How can one in personal contact with Jesus Christ live like that? It is possible because Christ is not simply a man who *lived,* but God who *lives* — dwelling in human hearts and giving stability, direction, strength, and purpose to life. His resources are unlimited. In Him are hid all the treasures of wisdom, all the secrets of science, all the design of the arts, all the knowledge of mankind. He was not merely a man doing His best for God, but God doing His best for men.

And what of the young people who follow him? They are afraid of no one or nothing, but have a clear-cut goal before them and a dynamic power dwelling within. These are the true world-changers of our day. These are the young revolutionaries who will never stop until every nation has been introduced to the greatest revolutionary this world will ever know — Jesus Christ.

DATE DUE

			PRINTED IN U.S.A.